Bust The Silos

Opening Your Organization For Growth

Hunter Hastings and Jeff Saperstein

Copyright © 2009 Hunter Hastings and Jeff Saperstein
All rights reserved.

ISBN: 1-4392-5972-0
ISBN-13: 9781439259726

Visit www.booksurge.com to order additional copies.

To Julie and Ilene

TABLE OF CONTENTS

List of Illustrations vii

List of Tables ix

Foreword xi

Preface xv

Acknowledgements xix

Introduction xxi

Part One: **The Idea of the Active Organization**

Chapter One   Value Creation Networks and Intangible Value 1

Chapter Two   Opening the Active Organization to Organic Growth ... 13

Chapter Three   Value Networks—Creating Growth Through
Innovating How We Work Together 23

Chapter Four   Developing Organic Organizations 31

Chapter Five   Transforming Sales and Marketing into
Demand Creation 41

Part Two: **The Transforming Power of the
Active Organization**

Chapter Six   How the Active Organization Learns—Genentech 51

Chapter Seven   How the Active Organization Creates New Value
via Global Customer Service—Cisco 69

Chapter Eight   How the Active Organization Uses Social Media to
Dialogue with The Customer—Wunderman 87

Chapter Nine   How the Active Organization Scales in Human
Networking—The Indus Entrepreneurs (TiE).103

Chapter Ten   How the Active Organization Creates a New Global
                   Business—Bumrungrad and Medical Tourism...121
Chapter Eleven   How the Traditional Organization
                   Transforms—Clorox 137

Afterword..147

About the Authors 149

LIST OF ILLUSTRATIONS

Figure 1-1   Replace structure with network to build
growth capability 10

Figure 6-1   Genentech: *How Do You Choose the Right Technology?* 60

Figure 6-2   Genentech: Future Integrated Solution 64

Figure 7-1   Cisco Value Network Mapping CIN with Pulse
Points for Monitoring and Focus................................81

Figure 7-2   Cisco Customer Interaction Network: Changes
What We Value and Measure..83

Figure 8-1   Wunderman Holistic Campaign Strategy 92

Figure 9-1   TiE Silicon Valley Charter Member, Member, and
Sponsor Profiles 105

Figure 10-1 International Cost Comparison for Medical Procedures....124

Figure 11-1 EMM Group Brand Building Framework 140

LIST OF TABLES

Table 1-1   Structure vs. Network 2

Table 1-2   Structure vs. Network: Value Assessment 8

Table 2-1   Transition from hierarchical to networked organization ...20

Table 7-1   Cisco Customer Interaction Network...............................77

FOREWORD

What would you do if you were given the opportunity to design a Demand Creation organization from scratch, unconstrained by historical legacy and unleashed from traditional thinking?

My team and I recently had the opportunity to do just that. The challenge was to develop new customers and consumers for products and brands they were unaware of in an existing category that had not seen much change for a long time. We had no requirement to follow historical norms of hierarchical structure and no pre-existing format to follow. We could design purely for Demand Creation.

Where to begin? We were veterans of old-style companies, so we knew many of the practices to avoid. We wanted to eliminate functional silos, where people in certain functions feel constrained from contributions across a wide swath of company issues and opportunities. We wanted to maximize the power of collaboration and to avoid the wasted energy of needless politics and disputes. We wanted to identify new ways to work with customers and distribution channels to find win-win solutions. We wanted to eliminate sources of internal friction. We wanted to be fast, nimble, and flexible to respond to our customers.

With this outlook, we made use of the most updated thinking and tools. By focusing on Demand Creation, we did not have to distinguish between marketing and sales in customer relationship management. These functions transformed into a new value network designed for maximum responsiveness to market needs. We were able to make R&D an integral part of Demand Creation rather than a separate activity, thereby avoiding all risk of dropping the ball between R&D and customer needs. We were able to integrate manufacturing into the Demand Creation thinking from the outset and establish a flexible logistics and manufacturing footprint designed to serve customer needs. We could scale more rapidly by plugging into an established global supply chain at multiple points with flexible supply options. Our factories became an adjunct to customer distribution centers, so we were able to design an innovative production and logistics solution to be more productive partners to our customers. Released from the traditional forms and constraints of organizational structure, we were liberated to innovate and improve profitability.

Our work with EMM Group has helped us integrate the thinking and best practices that are in this book. The breakthrough principles you will find here have proven very valuable in the organizational development for our business. Designing for Demand Creation, maximizing customer centricity, and organizing to integrate functions and geographies—in effect to Bust the Silos—has been integral to our success in a very price competitive, category stagnant marketplace.

Innovation is essential to achieve growth. Achieving these breakthroughs requires new ways of working and leveraging your knowledge, relationships and people assets. Today, the successful business leader must make these breakthroughs possible through purposeful changes in the organizational culture.

There must be a radical transformation of what is known as "marketing." Marketing must move to a holistic, system-wide approach that begins with insights and drives rapidly and relentlessly to the delivery of a better experience to consumers and channel customers in the marketplace. Similarly, we must totally re-think the concept of "sales" being mere transactions. Sales must become the customer-touching part of the same holistic Demand Creation system. *Bust the Silos* goes beyond the confines of marketing and sales to integrate all company functions and create a discipline built on collaborative processes, creativity, and measurement.

There are many books published on marketing and business. Most are weak adaptations of other peoples' thoughts. The authors of *Bust The Silos* have painstakingly probed and presented fresh insights and stories about successful adaptations by global leaders who can shed light for the rest of us on how to adopt technology for Demand Creation. The principles and practices illustrated in this book will help others to create the right mindset for change. All of us need to rethink how we deliver value to our shareholders, customer channels, and consumers, while transforming our organizations to be attractive to the best talent, both within and with outside partners. This book will help all of us steer our organizations through an increasingly challenging business environment. The authors have made a great contribution by clarifying a new advanced perspective. *Bust the Silos* will shape management thinking for a long time to come.

Philip Rundle, Chief Executive Officer, Mercury Paper

PREFACE

Most people in marketing departments, sales forces, innovation teams, strategy groups, R&D and IT functions have something in common. They have just been through a reorganization, are in the middle of a reorganization, or are just about to go through a reorganization. The old organization model for these functions no longer works; the jobs can't be done; the job descriptions are, at best, unable to keep up with change, or at worst, both meaningless and pointless.

If you are employed in marketing, it is likely you will soon be in a different position. The average tenure of a marketing director is about two years.

If you are employed in sales, you are probably feeling challenged by the increasing speed required to do business and the fast changing demands of new information technology, while wrestling with a changing compensation environment in which your company's policies are misaligned with the changing pricing, margins and competitiveness of the marketplace.

If you are employed in IT or finance, you are probably eternally frustrated by how difficult it is to incorporate the best practices for new systems into the actual decision-making of the divisions and departments in your corporation. Paradoxically, the demand for cost cutting and efficiency that technology can bring has never been greater, while the demand for increased customer responsiveness and innovation, which technology can deliver, continually runs up against organizational barriers to change.

Each department views their perspective through the lens of its function in the organization. Functions are often referred to as silos. The functional job description describes your responsibilities, accountabilities and tasks within your department; it may identify with whom you will interact and it may even describe some desirable attributes such as "leadership" and "teamwork".

The organization chart may indicate to whom you report, which department you're in, and whether your job position is deemed to be a peer, superior, or subordinate to others in your department.

However, none of this information about structure, hierarchy, titles and jobs can tell you the role you play in how the organization creates value and how you fulfill that role effectively. And in the modern, highly distributed, highly networked, collaborative enterprise—where value is created from intangibles rather than from materials and processing—roles are the way people work together for the systemic creation of value by the enterprise.

If this sounds familiar, then you know change must come.

Pitchforks ready? Good!

Now let's eliminate jobs and job descriptions, reporting hierarchies, functional departments, and silos!

In *Bust the Silos* we focus on the networked roles in multi-functional teams to create customer demand—Demand Creation—what we think of as the "front end" of the enterprise. This " moment of truth" is when we meet and engage customers, understand their needs, design an organizational response that serves that need, and create both a transaction and a relationship for revenue.

Traditionally, we may have called that set of roles by a functional name: "marketing," "sales," "customer management," or "channel management." But this excludes all the others who have a hand in making it possible to generate that revenue by contributing to the relationship with the customer: IT, operations, legal, finance, and support centers.

The hierarchical, departmental, job-delineated organization that we have known is no longer capable to meet the demands of the 21st century marketplace. Conventional job descriptions do not match how people actually create value when they work together supported by technology.

PREFACE

We can't be effective in Demand Creation trying to connect all these functional silos together. We need a new approach. We need to bust the silos!

The new approach we recommend—*Demand Creation*—replaces functional departments, false job descriptions and the high-friction ways of working we know and despise.

Bust the Silos: Opening Your Organization For Growth presents a conceptual framework and real-world examples of how to harness the capabilities of new productivity tools with new business processes for success. Simply, we must work differently: in roles, not just jobs; in multifunctional teams, not just departments; in networks, not just rigid structures; customer-centric, not just product centric; in listening to escalate responsiveness, not just communicating to get the message across.

The challenges we all face are to get ourselves ready to welcome change rather than react, to become porous rather than rigid, and to increase our collective intelligence for continuous improvement and innovation in an environment that is less predictable and more chaotic. This necessary transformation will affect the survival of individual organizations as well as the job satisfaction and productivity of the workforce.

So, let's bust those silos, remove those barriers, and transform our work with others to achieve breakthrough growth for our organizations and fulfillment for ourselves.

ACKNOWLEDGEMENTS

Many people have contributed their time, advice, perspective and good will to this book.

First, we want to acknowledge Gordon Wade, co-founder of EMM-Group and an active contributor and participant in this and every book in our series.

Thanks to Philip Rundle for his support and contributing the foreword.

Thanks to our assistants, Julie Moy Zelaya and Angela Woo Austria, for their dedication and diligence in research.

We owe a great debt to our interviewees, who graciously provided wisdom, experience, and perspective on their work: Verna Allee, Jamie Dinkelacker, Mark Ouyang, Harry Wittenberg, LaVeta Gibbs, Michael Joseph, Blake Park, Ajay Chopra, Raj Jaswa, Seshan Rammohan, Mayur Shah, Janice Gronveld, Kenneth Mays, and Doug Milliken.

In addition, we would like to thank David Sable, Andrew Sexton, Sat Duggal, and Betsy Farner.

Hunter Hastings and Jeff Saperstein

INTRODUCTION

"The way we work is our most important innovation"

— *Curt Carlson*

The productivity revolution of the last 25 years occurred in the organization of the supply chain. The next 25 years is about organizing the demand chain to ensure predictable, sustainable, profitable, long-term growth for global corporations. This book explains how to design organizations and processes that can make Demand Creation a scientific, process-based, predictable, repeatable management science.

Demand Creation is new. Before it emerged, companies would attempt—non-systematically—to drive demand by sending torrents of e-mails, paying for search engine advertising, trying to manage a sales funnel in CRM software, and/or investing millions of dollars behind unpredictable creative ideas for advertising and communications.

All these methods are old hat!

The new Demand Creation discipline is based on scientific processes to understand customer needs, translate these insights into innovation, and take the innovations to market effectively using repeatable systems, metrics and mathematical models. In addition, companies will innovate via new organizational designs to change how they operate internally across boundaries as well as externally with customers, collaborators and even competitors.

OPENING YOUR ORGANIZATION FOR GROWTH

The rise of the modern global corporation in the twentieth century created unprecedented wealth and regional power by leveraging a hierarchical organization comprising functional divisions and departments that operated in a mass production and distribution paradigm. Companies, such as Procter & Gamble in packaged goods and IBM in computer hardware, dominated their industries by creating the "gold standards" in practices to maximize profit based on these principles. The functions of R&D, Marketing, Sales, and Information Technologies (IT) emerged as distinctive competencies within their own "silos" and coordinated with other departments from within the walls of their silos as needed.

The most significant development for global corporations in the last quarter of the 20th Century was the transformation of the supply chain—creating "boundary-less" organizations and deploying technologies that can manage process for low cost, speed, flexibility and customer service operations, like Wal-Mart and Toyota.

In the first quarter of the 21st Century the most significant transformation will be a parallel effort on the demand side—driving top-line revenue growth organically through reliable, competitively advantaged Demand Creation systems that achieve the status of core capability. The convergence of R&D, marketing, sales and IT into a new function—the Demand Creation side of the enterprise—will be the focus of the next 20 years of enterprise development. It will require a different organization, new processes, new role definitions, and most significantly a customer (channel) and consumer (end purchaser/user) centric organization that will attract, retain, and partner with the customer/consumer in a profoundly different way than the centralized, hierarchical, functional, mass marketed and efficiency-focused corporation ever could.

Four profoundly significant business revolutions are coming together in a perfect storm of innovation: the digital revolution, a business process revolution, a business organization revolution and the Internet revolution. Successful companies will learn to reshape their R&D, marketing, sales and IT functions and job specifications within a new customer-centric organization paradigm to take account of these changes.

FROM INSIDE OUT TO OUTSIDE IN

The fundamental change is a reversal of the flow of the corporation from inside-out to outside-in. All the activities of the corporation that were outbound—R&D, sales, marketing, advertising, promotion, service centers—must now be reversed. The customer decides when they have a need and when they are ready to listen to information or receive a service from a company that might be able to meet that need. The company must restructure so it can anticipate and respond. We've never had a management science for this new paradigm. How successful companies and institutions are changing to meet this challenge is the core quest of our inquiry.

Inbound-outbound relationships must change, as must centralized/decentralized relationships. The center is no longer the locus of power in the organization, no longer where all-important decisions are made. The hierarchy no longer functions because Demand Creation decisions must be made at the bottom, rather than at the top. We need to engineer business processes and structures, metrics and technology to enable the decentralization of decisions by everyone in the organization to serve the consumer/customer.

The organization has to rethink strategy, structure, process and rewards. Management must now reconsider the kinds of people, processes, and rewards to get things right in opening the organization.

VALUE NETWORKS

There is a new organizational orientation that supports Demand Creation. Its technical name is Value Networks.

It focuses on the two kinds of value-creating power of relationships: one is between organization and the external environment—for example, with customers and suppliers; the second is internal—for example, between teams and teammates collaborating to meet customer needs.

The Value Networks orientation requires all members of an organization to have a system to serve customers at the moment thy want to be served in the way they want to be served. Any customer touchpoint and any customer event can be the occasion for service. Each member of the organization must understand his or her <u>role</u> in serving the customer and his or her <u>role</u> in collaborating with others for the same purpose. Everyone must know the <u>process</u> for serving the customer and the <u>process</u> for collaborating internally to do so. Each must understand the <u>knowledge</u> and data required for the purpose and how to collaborate together using that <u>knowledge</u>. And everyone must understand the <u>deliverable</u> to the customer as well as to internal colleagues.

Those elements—roles, processes, knowledge, and deliverables—define the interchanges within a Value Network. The new Active Organization must optimize these elements so that individuals and teams understand their collaborative roles, master the process, command the knowledge, and control deliverables.

There are several themes within *Bust the Silos* that we will explain and illustrate through the case studies we have selected. These are:

Roles rather than jobs: Most work will be collaborative with peers—inside and outside the organization—where roles are dynamically defined and linked by intangibles in the pursuit of deliverables and outcomes, rather than jobs that are statically defined by department and function (e.g., the marketing or sales manager). How people best work together transcends organization charts, lines of reporting, and functional responsibilities. Value networks that are permeable—inside and outside the organization—are the way work gets done. Mentors, coaches, and enablers become part of the organizational structure to continuously improve the collective intelligence and collaboration of the workforce. No longer should it be, "I will help you if I find the time," but rather, "It is my role to help you, so let's define the learning task together."

Intangible value creation, rather than just tangible deliverables: The old concept of value creation remains anchored in the model of capital assets. Companies used capital to invest in machines and created revenue by selling what the machines produced. In the second half of the 20th Century, we transitioned to intangible assets like software code and patents, but we continued to think and plan in terms of the revenue streams and cash flows generated by the assets.

In the 21st Century, value creation through intangibles takes on a new meaning. The intangibles that create value are operating ideas like the way we serve customers, the way we collaborate with companies outside our firewall, the way we work together, and the way we learn from each other: our processes, our spirit and our best practices. Learning is adaptation and knowledge creation. New tools and processes have made learning an integral part of continuous innovation to anticipate and exceed customer expectations.

In financial services in the 21st Century it will be our integrity and trust. In retail, it will be our collective trend monitoring sensitivity and the ability to integrate into networks of designers and suppliers to transform our trend knowledge into in-store or online presentation value. In industrial goods, it will be our ability to segment customers, understand the needs of different segments, and serve them with services wrapped around products that make them feel confident and comfortable in their relationship with us.

These are the new intangibles—you can't process map them, you can't patent them, you can't apply Six Sigma to them. But you must master them.

Multi-disciplinary collaborations replacing functional departments: The era of marketing, sales, IT, finance, all operating as fiefdoms with turf and territorial imperatives is closing—by necessity. Companies simply will not survive in a customer-centric marketplace where touch-point delivery of excellence is expected and dysfunctional internal organizational management gets in the way of value creation for the customer.

> *Multi-knowledgeable professionals are now more highly valued than specialists who are narrow and deep.* We all have to learn and know more than what we thought we needed to know when we take on a job. If we do not have the specific expertise at hand, we have to know where to find it and how to work with those people who have it.

Permeable organizations are more successful than verticals. Project teams have to work without borders through geographically dispersed colleagues, vendors, consultants, research labs, and communications firms. Technology enables virtual workforces; organizations must adapt to provide these virtual workforces what they need to create value for profitable growth.

The innovation organization has to respond to constant change and unpredictability, not static, predictable workflow-processes. The experience curve and workflow process charts so popular twenty years ago have become albatrosses around the necks of management who need to build into the workflow continuous innovation and response to constant exception and change.

All organizational roles we play must be customer centric to provide excellence at each touch-point. Basically, the creation of value rests on the relationship with the consumer and customer. Everyone needs to work towards the fulfillment of excellence in Demand Creation, and that requires a level of customization, insight, innovation, business processes, metrics, and the use of technology that has not hitherto been mastered in the old-fashioned hierarchical organization.

We can see the emergence of this transformation quite simply through this typical scenario.

Consider the difference between the counter personnel for some airlines compared with others. To the consumer, the personnel are the airline. Well, you could say, counter personnel are not marketers or salespeople; they are counter personnel. But no, they become the airline, because they are the people who touch the consumer to make something go right or wrong and they can really influence attitudes.

Imagine Mr. Jones arrives to the airport early and he wants to get on a different flight, so he can get home a few hours earlier. He tells the counter person he had a ticket for a later plane, but would like to be placed on this earlier flight. The counter person looks down at her computer screen and she begins to do all the magic. She says, "Okay, let me tell you what I can do. I think I can put you in an exit row seat and keep the next seat empty." So, now Mr. Jones not only gets to take an earlier flight, but he will have more legroom than anyone else in coach. That counter person is an important part of Demand Creation. She has touched Mr. Jones by solving his problem and has used her ability to have a positive effect on him.

This is "the moment of truth". It occurs at different places at different times. The president of the airline company is much less capable of affecting that moment of truth than a stewardess or a ramp worker. However, for the moment of truth to become positive for customers as standard operating procedure requires a whole organizational shift: job training, business processes, use of technology, and integration of marketing and sales. This can only happen with a strategic commitment to become a Demand Creation corporation.

What happened in the airline case was that IT enabled that counter person to know who Mr. Jones is, to know which seats were available on that aircraft, and to know she had the authority and capability to give Mr. Jones that seat. IT enabled her to recognize Mr. Jones, to create a series of options for him, and to implement those options right on the spot.

Customer-centric training empowered her to make decisions and changes to meet the customer's need. Edge-of-the-network organization made it unnecessary for her to ask permission from a higher role in the hierarchy. The finance department had approved pre-determined pricing algorithms so she did not need to call them. All of these active-organization transactions were required to work smoothly to put a smile on Mr. Jones' face.

To achieve this anecdotal "moment of truth" requires a management commitment to opening the organization to become a customer centric, active organization for people to work in roles, through multifunctional teams, networked through technology to be able to improvise with the principles of Demand Creation.

This book provides the vision to fuse Finance, R&D, Marketing, Sales, IT, and Learning and Development into a process-driven, technology-enabled, demand-side discipline, connecting it to measurable improvements in brand equity, share, margin and volume. It introduces the marketing mind-set to help everyone in the organization to apply Demand Creation principles to ensure outstanding customer/consumer satisfaction—the source for organic top-line growth that all successful corporations will need to master to thrive in the 21st century.

To illustrate these principles we have researched companies and organizations that have successfully implemented the *Bust the Silos* principles and we have conducted extensive interviews with some of the best practitioners in their fields. We chose a wide variety of industries and geographies to show how universally these concepts are being applied. We edited our interviews with "best practitioners" but retained their own words, passion, and experiences in extended excerpts so you can hear from the best what they have learned: the mistakes to avoid, the problems encountered, the wisdom and lessons learned.

Accordingly, the book is organized into two sections.

Part One is our conceptual framework. Chapter 1 introduces a key idea: thinking about organization as a network rather than a hierarchical structure. This is the critical first step, since it rids us of jobs and job descriptions, functional silos and other barriers to growth. We introduce Demand Creation as a special kind of networked organization. Chapter 2 demonstrates the idea of the Active Organization that network thinking makes possible: fast-changing, adaptive, and collaborative. Chapter 3 provides more detail on Value Networks, an important enabler of the Active Organization. Chapter 4 provides highly relevant examples (Google and Toyota) of how the active organization puts teams to work to innovate in software and eliminate waste. Chapter 5 focuses on a key element of the Demand Creation network: how Sales, Marketing and IT are integrated to serve customers.

Part Two employs a wide range of case histories from a wide variety of industries, geographies, and disciplines to illustrate our concepts. Chapter 6 illustrates the network power of a contemporary learning organization: Genentech. Chapter 7 employs an example of global networked integration in the service of customer relationships and innovation at Cisco. Chapter 8 shows how recently invented tools in social media are applied to improve customer relationships for complex business software from Microsoft by expert practitioners at Wunderman. Chapter 9 illustrates the power of global networking in the service of individual entrepreneurs in start-ups via The Indus Entrepreneurs. Chapter 10 shows how the networked organizational approach can create an entire new class of business – medical destination tourism at Bumrungrad International Hospital in Thailand. And Chapter 11 shows how the contemporary ideas of Demand Creation and networked organizational thinking can be applied to more traditional companies, as demonstrated by The Clorox Company.

Our hope is that each viewpoint and story will be fresh, informative, compelling, and useful in helping you apply the principles and practices of Demand Creation to your own business. Most of all, we hope to provide some impetus in your company towards busting silos, breaking down barriers, eliminating departments, blowing up organization charts and creating a new, open, collaborative, free-flowing growth engine.

Part One: The Idea of the Active Organization

CHAPTER ONE
VALUE CREATION NETWORKS AND INTANGIBLE VALUE

▶ What is the difference between conventional organizational structures and value networks?

▶ What is the difference between roles and jobs?

▶ How do intangibles create value?

▶ How can Management encourage the value creation from intangibles?

———

"The customer can't be the center of your business if you organize by silos. The curse of the functionally organized business is that each function has its own goals, metrics, mind-sets, and reward systems."[1]

"Integrating the functions to serve customers is what makes good execution possible. It's the hardest imperative to achieve if it's not already designed into the firm and living in the culture. Integration demands organization-wide clarity about external and internal realities, along with clearly shared values and priorities, an appropriate organization design, supportive systems and processes, the right human resources, cross-functional teamwork, and common reward criteria."[2]

— *Neal Capon*

Companies of all sizes exist to create value. They must create value for customers. That's why customers buy the goods and services the company sells. We'll define the value proposition later in this book.

---

1   Capon, Noel. <u>The Marketing Mavens</u>. New York: Crown Business, 2007: 38
2   Capon, Noel. <u>The Marketing Mavens</u>. New York: Crown Business, 2007: 39

But first, we must examine how companies do the work that results in value creation. We must recognize that the old form of organization—the old way work used to get done—has run out of steam and a new way is emerging.

The emergent organization is called the Value Creation Network.
Table 1-1 defines the component differences between the old 20th century organization structure and the new 21st century network:

Organization Structure	Network
Jobs	Roles
Hierarchy	Collaboration
Functions	Deliverables

Table 1-1 Structure vs. Network

Jobs are the building blocks of the structure. When you join a corporation, you are given a job and a job description. The job description defines which tasks you are allotted and what responsibilities you have. But it seldom describes how you contribute to the transformation of the assets of the corporation—its knowledge, information, processes, and methods.

Jobs are grouped in a function, such as Marketing, Sales, Operations, Finance or Legal. This functional organization solidifies specialization; job-holders are subject matter experts. They are defined by their function. Most frequently, they are promoted within their function, but seldom do they move into another function. Sure, we all know of lawyers who have become CEO's and salespeople who have become marketers. But mostly we think in terms of the ascendant career in the function – the ultimate achievement of the marketer is to become Chief Marketing Officer, of the lawyer to become Chief Counsel, and of the financial analyst to become Chief Financial Officer.

And the very concept of "Chief this" and "Chief that" reveals the key structural device of the organization: the hierarchy. You start at the bottom and work your way up to the top. You report to a superior, who assesses your job performance. You are not customer-centric; you are boss-centric.

VALUE CREATION NETWORKS AND INTANGIBLE VALUE 3

You succeed by pleasing your superiors; you are rewarded when your superiors say you are doing a good job.

Jobs in functions and functional hierarchies are captured in the organization chart. It's home base for you—you can find where you are located, like a conference room on a building diagram or a line item on a database. You know what level you have reached and what the next level is that you aspire to. You govern your business life by assessing where you are in the hierarchy relative to where you want to be and where your reference individuals are.

None of this organization design and structure is about value creation. It's about how those in charge can give orders to the people who work in the organization and expect that their orders will be followed. If we tell the person at the next step below us in the hierarchy, that person will tell the next one down and so on and so on until someone does something.

THE NETWORKED ORGANIZATION

Patricia Seybold, author of <u>Outside Innovation</u> suggests that the organizational structure is well ingrained in most corporate cultures and is part of human nature.

"No matter how fast you want to move, human nature is going to get in the way. It's not about a particular type of person, because everybody usually has a lot of goodwill. It's trying to figure out what are really the best ways to get information flowing across these functional silos and try to get everybody seeing things the same way...What happens is that in many organizations there is a degree of inertia.... And you can come up with as many blueprints as you want – top-down leadership, customer champions, road maps for how to do things – but the fact of the matter is they're only going to work at the pace at which the organization's culture is able to absorb them."[3]

As opposed to jobs in functions in hierarchies, the networked organization starts from the idea of roles. Everyone in the organization can identify their role in the value creation process: how they contribute to the purpose of the enterprise.

---

3   Conversations with Marketing Masters, Mazor and Miles, John Wiley & Sons, 2007 (p 184);

Here is an actual example from a major global corporation we worked with, masked for confidentiality. The company tried to drive innovation and growth by putting the customer at the center of all innovation processes.

This was a laudable goal since insights—deep understanding of the motivations that drive customer behavior—can create new growth streams as an input to innovation. They created the job of Customer Insights Manager in the business units.

The next stage was to bring in the HR function to define the job responsibilities and tasks to be done, and to specify the qualifications and experience that candidates must have to qualify for the job. The HR function generated a job description of tasks, responsibilities and qualifications, and a reporting hierarchy indicating the manager to whom this new job reported in the organizational structure. The company created and filled the new positions. There was a flurry of initial activity and allocation of budget resources to generating new customer understanding through segmentation studies and other research techniques, and Insights Workshops to generate real customer insights. The insights were transferred to the R&D function and to the Marketing function as input to their processes.

But then two barriers to value creation arose. First, the process driven by R&D to develop new products did not produce the right kinds of innovations; there were too many small ideas and they tended to be continuous improvements rather than step changes or major leaps forward. Second, the process driven by Marketing to communicate with the consumer produced a similar result—more of the same that's a little bit better, rather than innovative ways to engage with customers and create a new basis for customer relationships.

Meanwhile, the Customer Insights Managers became dismayed and frustrated. They did a good job of generating insights but did not see those insights turned into demand-generating innovation and, worse, were given no role in the downstream commercialization of their insights. In the world of process-based organization, the right hand-offs were made from the insights generation function to the R&D function and to the marketing function. But in the world of value creation, this was not producing the required results.

VALUE CREATION NETWORKS AND INTANGIBLE VALUE   5

If the company management had thought of Customer Insights as a role instead of a job, they would have redefined the overall role as Insights Generation. This would include an *Insights—to—Innovation* role of working with R&D to transform the insight into product ideas and commercialize them. It would also include an *Insights-to-Brand Building* role to work with marketing to transform the insight into stronger and more productive customer relationships. These roles are defined by exchanging results and assessment information with another role to improve future outputs. Such a role-based view defines much more clearly the value contribution that the individual is making than does the job description of "Customer Insights Manager."

Don Schultz, professor of Integrated Marketing Communications at the Medill School of Journalism, Northwestern University, provides some useful insight on this issue.

Basically, functional specialists don't like change. We know that if you have customers, it's not the marketing people who have all the impact on them. It's also the financial people, the HR people, the operations people—it's across the board. It's an organizational thing.

The problem, I find, is that too many marketing people want to be a functional group inside the organization. But that marginalizes marketing's role. Because if you say that marketing is responsible for customers and communication, it allows the rest of the organization to say: 'OK, we don't have to worry about customers at all. That's marketing's job. So we don't have to worry about how product quality or customer service or delivery times impact customers. That's marketing's responsibility.'[4]

ROLES ARE FAR MORE EMPOWERING CONCEPTS THAN JOBS

Roles are defined not as positions in a hierarchy, but by interactions with others. A role is a collaborative concept. In a job I must complete a set of tasks. In a role, I must figure out how to work with others effectively to achieve the value creation result. In job-based hierarchies, we often hear about the problems of "politics" and about the difficulty of performing

---

4   Conversations with Marketing Masters, Mazor and Miles, John Wiley & Sons, 2007 (p 168);

"across silos." That's a result of the creation of functional hierarchies in organization charts.

"Politics" is the Failure to Collaborate!

In a role-based organization, collaboration is the whole point. Roles are defined by effective interactions with others.

And the medium of interaction is the exchange. In my role, I collaborate with other roles by providing an output that the collaborator requires in order to perform their role. The exchange could be called a deliverable—usually an intangible one. It might be processed information or an analysis; it might be a strategy that the next role turns into plans and initiatives. The organizational implication of the collaborative nature of roles—and the exchange of intangibles between roles—is that accountability is horizontal.

By contrast, in the conventional organizational hierarchy, accountability is vertical. You are told what to do by your boss and your boss assesses whether you performed the defined task satisfactorily. In the collaborative network of roles, accountability is horizontal—to other people who require deliverables from you. Accountability changes from an assessment of your performance by a superior to an objective measurement of whether your role delivered value or not.

This is a radical change in the nature of work whose implications we will illustrate through chapters three, four, and five and the case studies with interviews in Part Two of the book.

The Role of Intangibles: How They Create Value

The second major change in value creation is that intangibles create value. We've long known there is a role for intangibles in the corporation. What we might call the "bedrock" theory of business was that assets were the source of value, and the amount of value that was created could be captured by calculating a return on assets (factories, buildings and piles of capital) or return on investment.

Value Creation Networks and Intangible Value

Today we understand that assets can also be intangibles. The first [no]tion was probably centered on the idea of patents—pieces of intellec[tual] property that could be codified, certified by the government, and competi[-]tively protected so that the inventor of the intangible could benefit from it without sharing it. For a long time, business theorists got tangled up in the calculation of the value of intangible assets. Since factories and buildings could be valued, it stands to reason that patents and other intangibles could be valued. So we spent a lot of energy doing so.

Now we realize that the important question is not, "What is the value of intangible assets?" but rather, "How do intangible assets create new value?" That's a harder question to answer, and it is made even harder by the fact that we have now identified a much greater range of intangible assets that can create value. The range includes brands, processes, information, reputation, corporate cultures and even work processes.

Essentially, value is created when a role completes a deliverable for another role to use. The deliverable can be an intangible output (such as an insight into customer behavior and motivations). But it must also be wrapped up in an enabling intangible, which could be a process or a framework. The enabling intangible tells the recipient what to do next when they receive the deliverable.

Here's an example. Let's refer back to the Customer Insights role we mentioned earlier in this chapter. Suppose that role completes the generation of an insight. They hand it on to three recipients: R&D, Customer Solutions and Strategic Planning. For the R&D recipient, the insight must be handed over in the context of the Insights-to-Innovation process, so that R&D knows how to plug the insight into the product research and development process, so that a better innovation idea emerges as the result of the insight.

For the Customer Solutions recipient, the commercialization and communications process must enable the insight, so that Customer Solutions can leverage the insight into a solution (and the story of the solution) that's of benefit to the customer.

8 BUST THE SILOS

For the Strategic Planning recipient, the insight must be wrapped into the strategic planning process, to inform the development of the five-year-plan and to allocate resources most intelligently.

In each of these cases, if a process did not accompany the insight, the recipient would be unsure how to use it and no value would be created. When the insight is enabled by the process, the result is a focused effort driving toward an end result of value to the customer: a new innovation that capitalizes on the insight, a new solution where the innovation is combined with others and with the appropriate information to maximize its benefit to the customer, and a new strategic plan to allocate resources to make the most value out of the insight as possible. Table 1-2 defines the differences between structure and network to create value.

Intangible assets have value	Intangible assets create value
Protect and patent my assets	How widely can we share the asset among value-creating collaborators
I've done my job when I have created a valuable output	My role is part of an end-to-end process; when I hand over to the next role, I must provide a deliverable and an enabler for the next step
I focus on my output	I focus on the creation of customer value and all the steps between me and that end result

Table 1-2 Structure vs. Network: Value Assessment

Intangibles create value by combining new deliverables (ideas, insights, innovations, plans, communications) with the appropriate enabling process. The ultimate receiver is the customer, who receives a solution that may include some tangible assets (such as a product) and a whole lot of enabling intangibles (such as the sales process, the communications process, the relationship management process, training, servicing, and many more). In opening the organization to create networks of roles and multi-functional teams, management can unleash expertise and creativity for innovative solutions that will increase growth.

The Demand Creation Network

The organization looks very different when viewed from the perspective of how it creates value, rather than how it is structured. The vertical hierarchy and specialist functional job pillars do not create value; collaboration between people playing roles and utilizing processes and other intangibles is what creates value.

The key roles and processes in the Demand Creation Network are:

The Customer

Everything begins with the customer. The customer provides all the energy in the Demand Creation network. The customer provides the first input—information about their needs. The Demand Creation enterprise can get this information through research, behavior observation, analysis of click stream data, or other data. Usually the customer freely gives it (we will see this illustrated in the Wunderman/Microsoft and Cisco case studies). The customer also provides the final output of the Demand Creation system by giving revenue to the enterprise in return for goods and services that meet their needs and deliver value.

Insights Generation

The first process of the enterprise is to collect and interpret the data from the customer. The data is turned into knowledge, understanding and insights. It now has more value because it can be passed on as a deliverable from the analytics role to the innovation role.

The highest value form in which the data is passed on is an insight. An insight is defined as a deep understanding of customer needs and the motivations that drive their behavior. If we understand this, then we are in a strong position to define future (or unmet) needs and to anticipate customer behavior if we were to develop a new solution to meet future needs.

10 BUST THE SILOS

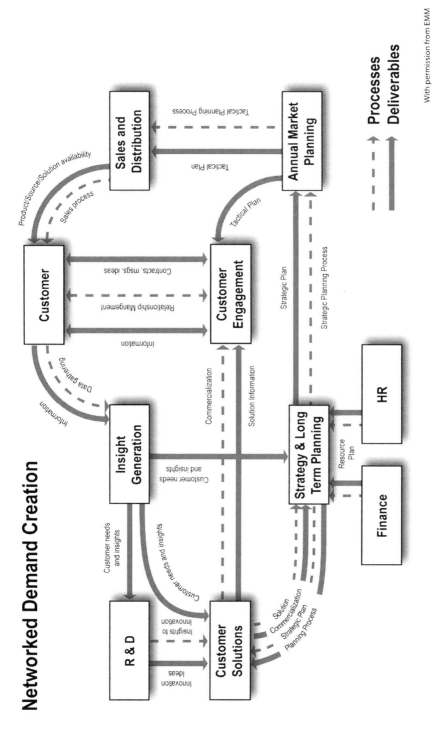

Figure 1-1 Replace structure with network to build growth capability

Innovation R&D

Innovation is the translation of customer knowledge into new ideas to meet customer needs. Here, customer knowledge might be combined with scientific knowledge to create new products, or with historical information and external information to create new patterns and solutions.

Strategy

Strategy identifies the best customers to serve, the solution area in which to serve them and the competitors to beat to become the preferred supplier. Strategy is a user of information from those nodes on the Demand Creation Network that touch the customer, and a supplier of deliverables (Strategies) to the rest of the network.

Planning

Planning helps all the parts of the Demand Creation Network to allocate resources efficiently and effectively. When planning is a role, rather than a job, it represents the communal resource allocation choices of the collaborative network. When it is a job, it tends to become a hated restrictor of resources as seen from the point of view of other jobs.

Delivery

Nothing happens until the customer takes delivery and money changes hands in a transaction. Whether it is a salesforce or a website, delivery is a critical role in the Demand Creation Network. This role must be as equally connected and equally informed as all others.

DEMAND CREATION: A SPECIFIC KIND
OF VALUE-CREATION NETWORK

The most important value-creation network in the enterprise is Demand Creation. In the past, we would have used a term like Marketing, or Product Marketing, or Sales or Customer Management.

With Demand Creation we see the continuous, seamless linkage among Marketing, Customer Management, R&D and Product Development. Feedback from the customer and the market provides the R&D team with the data it needs to create and develop new products. Similarly, feedback about the logistical needs of the customer is information that Operations uses to improve service. These activities—the exchange of information to improve deliverables—create value. They build the relationship capital of the enterprise and they generate revenue in the continued and expanded exchange of goods and services. The ultimate output is growth—of the enterprise, of the level of exchange with customers, and ultimately of the economy in which they operate and collaborate together.

Purposeful growth is the only outcome that matters. Whether it is the growth of GDP, the growth of global trade, or the growth of jobs, we are pleased when growth occurs and disappointed when growth stagnates or reverses. Growth is the important metric as the indicator of success: for our careers, our enterprise, our economy, and our world.

Growth starts from Demand Creation. Without demand there is no growth. Without increasing demand, there is no continuous improvement. Our purpose in this book is to identify the keys to successful Demand Creation and how to bust the silos to open the organization for growth.

Chapter Two
Opening the Active Organization to Organic Growth

▶ Why does hierarchical organizational structure hinder customer responsiveness?

▶ How does an organization change to be more customer-responsive?

▶ How do networks function in an Active Organization?

The most creative individuals, teams and organizations are extremely disciplined. But it is a special kind of discipline—one that unleashes creativity in the service of developing important innovations.

— Curt Carlson

The Emergence of the Active Organization

The modern corporation, modeled on companies such as General Motors and Procter & Gamble, became the organizational paradigm for the last half of the 20th century, enabling the Developed World to provide unparalleled societal wealth and affluence. Organizational strategy reflected a focus on mass production, mass distribution and mass consumption.

The organizational design process for this strategy brought us the hierarchical organization structure, the matrixed organization, and tools like strategy-structure alignment.

Today, traditional organizational design cannot keep pace with the demands of the fast moving marketplace. Organizations must open their organizational processes and designs to respond to daily market changes. They must be active and continuously changing.

The old order – still existing in many companies—is the hierarchical organization chart. Like the military, it's designed to give, transmit, receive and act on orders from the top. Organizing in silos, management transmits orders to be efficiently channeled in a vertical path from top to bottom. The infantry needs to march when told to march, and we don't want to confuse the pilots who fly the airplanes with an order to march.

Many corporations adopted this efficient military organization, because they observed how it made complex operations work. Therefore, they built their top-to-bottom silos designed for order transmission. They were run with an iron rule from the CEO and Vice Presidents. Annual plans were handed down for execution. From the end of WWII through the last decade of the 20th century, economic growth and centrally directed technological innovation were sufficient to drive enterprise growth. No longer!

Tellingly, there is no customer for the military. The military organization is not customer-oriented. It does not seek feedback. As we entered a new century, many far-sighted CEO's recognized that they needed to think harder about customers, understand their needs better, be more responsive, and compete on how well they were served. This is "customer-centricity." But to become customer centric, management has to eliminate the silos—both within and external to the organization.

CUSTOMERS HAVE A NEED TO BUY SOLUTIONS, NOT PRODUCTS OR SERVICES.

Large tech companies like IBM and HP illustrate this change. Louis P. Gerstner, author of <u>Who Says Elephants Can't Dance? Inside IBM's Historic Turnaround</u>, explained that customers were faced with the need to solve complex information technology, data analysis, data-sharing and decision-support problems. IBM was organized in silos: one division to sell the customer mainframes; another division to sell servers; and yet another to sell software. Multiple IBM divisions called on a single customer to sell them products. IBM was not organized to ask customers about the problems they were trying to solve and opportunities they were trying to seize and then design solutions that crossed IBM silos to offer them a single solution. Yet, this is what IBM's customers needed and yearned for.

OPENING THE ACTIVE ORGANIZATION TO ORGANIC GROWTH   15

Gerstner identified this need by simply talking to customers. But he did it in a way no one from within the silo'd organization could—with no commitments to products or product-based revenue or to preconceived plans or to bosses. He identified what A. G. Lafley, CEO of Procter & Gamble from 2002–2009, has since confirmed as the role only the CEO can play. He brought the "realistic outside" back to the organization and informed the organization what the customers really wanted.[5]

At the time, there was no organizational design to achieve the desired solution. In fact, there were calls to break up IBM, indicating that no one could conceive of the appropriate organizational design. Gerstner originated it. The new IBM became an early (and extremely effective) example of the networked organization. It was defined by common corporate goals (like customer satisfaction, solution selling and the enhancement of the IBM brand equity), busting silos, and replacing the silo walls with horizontal organizational mechanisms like cross-functional teams and solution-design collaborations.

One simple example can tell the story. The old IBM organization was silo'd by country. Country managers maintained customer contact with customer installations in their country, which often affected product/service mix, price and other attributes of the customer offering. The multinational customer might prefer to deal with IBM on a different level to obtain consistent pricing and offerings. Therefore, Gerstner decreed that IBM organization starts at the customer level, with customer teams, customer offerings and so on. There was tremendous in-built resistance (not least because of incentive systems, but also because of power bases, and the desire to maintain established functionality built around the country organization) that required a strong CEO mandate to overcome. Because of Gerstner's leadership, and, of course, because of continued customer-centric evolution since then, IBM exemplifies the ability to identify customer needs and meet them with complex tailored solutions on the global stage.

Many other companies have evolved towards becoming a customer-centric organization. There are new standard organizational designs that capture the power and energy of customer-centricity. One example is the

---

5   "What Only the CEO Can DO" A.G. Lafley, Harvard Business Review, May 2009

front-back organization.[6] At the risk of over-simplification, the "front" is customer-touching and charged with understanding customer needs; the "back" is design-and-development oriented, charged with coming up with customer solutions to meet the identified needs. The "front" and the "back" are linked by processes for gathering customer intelligence, processing it, designing solutions, and energizing the various parts of the company to collaborate in delivering the solution.

Cross-functional teams, collaborative software for information sharing, and customer-centric metrics systems has proven to be effective. However, they are still theoretical structures that are grand designs, prepared by experts and frequently imposed on the organization in monumental (and often monumentally disruptive) change management projects. Change management is still essentially a top-down concept.

Peter Drucker said that it is impossible to manage change. The best you can do is prepare for it and try to stay ahead of it. He suggested that " seeing and creating white space" would be one of management's major challenges ahead.

Management in the twenty-first century faces fundamental changes in the size and scope of opportunities. Businesses have historically defined "opportunity" as a chance to capture market share and rake in high profits through greater productivity, a new and improved product or service, the acquisition of a competitor, or expansion into a new territory. But increasingly, opportunity is all about seeing, or even creating, white space—uncharted markets that can be identified only by looking hard at both the external environment and the numerous unsatisfied demands of increasingly informed customers. Truly innovative products and services create their own markets.[7]

Today, organizations are emerging that are capable of living up to Drucker's dictum. We use the term "emerging" carefully—it has not been imposed, it has self-generated. That's why we call it the "Active Organization."

---

6   "Designing the Customer-Centric Organization", Jay Galbraith, Jossey-Bass, 2005

7   The Definitive Drucker: Challenges for Tomorrow's Executives, Elizabeth Edersheim, McGraw-Hill, 2007, (page 5)

THE ACTIVE ORGANIZATION

The customer remains the driver of the Active Organization. Companies exist only to create and serve customers. Three major innovation vectors drive the new organizational form:

1. The evolution of network thinking as an organizational metaphor.

2. The speed of change that accelerates to a speed that cannot be actively managed, but must be encouraged via automatic enablers and accommodated via auto-response mechanisms.

3. The collaborative communications technology that implements speed and connections in new ways, using the 24 hours of the day and the geographically dispersed talent of the corporation with unprecedented productivity, so long as organizational structure does not get in the way.

HOW NETWORKS OPERATE

Let's think about networks. They have no hierarchical governing structure: everything is joined to everything; everyone can talk with everyone. Users can enhance networks (e.g., by adding information) and networks can automatically respond to users (e.g., by detecting patterns of usage and automatically suggesting new offerings based on those patterns). The edge of the network is the key locus of information gathering, interaction with users, and the delivery of services. The edge of the network is not always operated by the same company as the center—in a communications network, AT&T can deliver service through handsets designed and manufactured by others, sold by independent vendors, and owned (possibly in the context of a service contract) by the user. In the context of roaming, the AT&T network links with another network to provide service at the edge. The center and internal hubs provide enablement through hardware, software, services, and algorithms. Innovation—in response to the data collected at the edge and agglomerated in the center—is loaded at the center and deployed to the edge. The edge determines whether the innovation is useful and, therefore, successful.

Now think about the organization as a network. The edge is the contact between the company and the customer. The customer draws down services (such as sales and service, delivery, maintenance, upgrades) on demand. He prefers a single and consistent interface to do so, in order to operate efficiently on the basis of best practice, non-variable standards. He wants to be able to connect to the "right" resource within his supplier at the right time to get the right response from a single instance of contact with no handoffs and minimal delay. He wants to be able to make special requests that he knows can't be accommodated instantly, but prefers faster to slower, with the solution coming back to him from the same single contact with which the request was initiated. The edge dictates how the network must be enabled to respond.

Within the network, the hubs and the center must be designed to enable the edge to respond appropriately. It's why the center and the hubs exist— the global headquarters and the regional offices and the research infrastructure and the HR function and all the elements we traditionally think of as the solid furniture of an organization. They exist only to empower the edge—the interface with the customer.

There can be no hierarchy in a successful network. There must be only enough structure to enable flexibility and responsiveness. Everything must be connected to everything and everyone to everyone, and information and ideas must flow freely. What kinds of organizational elements get in the way of this?

- ▶ Jobs: What if an information request comes from a customer to the "wrong" person—the one who says, "It's not my job"? At minimum there's delay and a loss of speed; at worst, there's a lost customer.

- ▶ Silos: What if there is a need for an idea to solve a problem in Germany and there's an individual with an answer in Ukraine because they've seen the problem before. The country silos may not allow the request to cross the silo wall or the answer to come back.

- ▶ Hierarchy: What if an individual has a contribution to make to a service that's conducted higher in the organization, but is not called upon because he/she has not reached the right level in the hierarchy? The chance for an improvement may be lost or impaired or delayed.

OPENING THE ACTIVE ORGANIZATION TO ORGANIC GROWTH   19

The active organization breaks out of these constraints. It becomes a global network of talent motivated and mobilized to solve problems, improve products and turn new ideas into action. It makes experience and knowledge a global commodity that can be applied anywhere in the system to solve any problem. (See Chapter Seven on Cisco Customer Interaction Network for more on how these principles can be implemented.)

The network knows what talent is connected to it as its resource and what knowledge it has access to and can share. The network matches problem specifications to the right talent and knowledge, and individuals self-select to collaborate on the solutions. The organization ceases to be one of countries and departments and functions and jobs and levels and becomes a global swarm of networked talent. The organization no longer faces a weakness that its executives in Ecuador do not have the experience of those in Japan—it is truly global in its use of experience. It no longer has the issue of different service levels in different divisions; if that ever happens, the global talent team applies the global knowledge to fix the local problem.

There are some early indicators of this emerging active organization. IBM has its global Idea Jam. It is a period of time in which IBM'ers all over the world contribute their thinking, ideas and suggestions to solve challenging problems of the present and future for the corporation. A giant global blog and a white board collect and combine all contributions. There is no respect for hierarchy, rank, geographical location, job, division or silo. All contributions are equal in their source and are used or not used purely on the basis of their utility, originality and applicability to the problem or opportunity at hand. It's global, boundary-less, and talent-based and knowledge-based.

Procter & Gamble's Connect and Develop system for product and technology innovation is another example. P&G identifies the consumer's unmet needs, and then makes a request to their connect-and-develop network for ideas, technologies and other contributions to meet those needs. The network is a set of connections to scientists, alumni, universities, suppliers, and all P&G countries and anyone who could possibly have a contribution, idea or technology. P&G recognizes that all the knowledge cannot possibly be contained within P&G so the connect-and-develop network is 100% open, and constantly expanding at the edge with more connections for greater reach. There is a center to the network in the global HQ and a series of regional hubs.

Each regional hub is free to add its own set of connections to universities, laboratories, suppliers and thinkers, and the network grows as an increasing amount of knowledge hums through it and more solutions emerge from it.

In a more focused way, Genentech has developed a process for informal learning for salespeople. When a new drug is launched, Genentech sets up a Wiki, so salespeople can post questions from the field that are answered by a team of experts. All questions and answers are collected, categorized and posted so within a few months a unique body of knowledge is created and shared by all (See Chapter Six on Genentech). Opportunity can be unleashed when the organization ceases to be hierarchical and becomes a global knowledge and talent network. Four changes can unleash the flood.

From	To
Jobs	Roles – individuals can play multiple roles as members of different mini-networks in the global network, e.g. country brand managers, members of the global brand management community and members of the innovation network. They have no boss, and are accountable to each of the networks for their collaborative contribution.
Silos	Global problem solving networked teams – individuals are no longer constrained to contributing only in their country, or in their function, or in their division. They are called upon by the network for their contribution and they can call on the network for contributions.
Hierarchy	Connectedness – Individuals are not told by their boss what to do or assessed by thier boss on how well they do it. They are connected to the network and selected by the network (or self select) because their talent and experience match the specifications of a problem-solution need.
Career progression – talent is moved to location of the job	Knowledge accumulation – knowledge and experience are accumulated by individuals and the network calls on those individuals for new and more and more valuable contributions.

Table 2-1 Transition from hierarchical to networked organization

Summary

▶ 21st Century enterprises must be organized as customer solutions-based rather than silo-based along country, product division or department demarcation lines.

▶ Organizations must become networked and role-focused, rather than hierarchical and job-focused, to succeed.

▶ Speed in response has become the new equity for corporations.

Chapter Three
Value Networks — Creating Growth through Innovating How We Work Together

▶ How do we define roles and not just jobs?

▶ How can we integrate departments such as sales and marketing within a value network?

▶ How do intangibles create value?

How can people and computers be connected so that collectively they act more intelligently than any person, group or computer?

—*Tom Malone*

We have all experienced the profound truth that certain projects, organizations, or multi-discipline teams just work better than others. Even if the resources, resumes, project descriptions, and circumstances are the same, the way people seem to "click" is a variable that makes all the difference. Understanding how to use technology and business processes is necessary, but insufficient to account for the difference. The way groups work together—formally and informally—creates or destroys value.

Relationships between people inside and outside an enterprise create economic value by sharing today's knowledge and generating new knowledge. Value networks are a new form of organizational design thinking based on human interdependence. Companies have both external and internal value networks: external networks include customers, intermediaries, stakeholders, open innovation networks and suppliers; internal value networks focus on key activities, processes and relationships that cut across functional departments, such as order fulfillment, innovation, lead processing, or customer support. Value is created through exchanges and the relationships between roles that advance innovation and wealth; it is the source of company growth and success.

Verna Allee is one of the global experts on Value Networks.

In her book, <u>The Future of Knowledge: Increasing Prosperity through Value Networks</u>, she describes Value Network Analysis, a systems mapping and analysis approach to understanding tangible and intangible value creation in an enterprise. Value Network Analysis provides a standard way to define, map and analyze the roles and participants, transactions, and tangible and intangible deliverables that together form a value network.

It may be useful to define tangible and intangible value. Tangible value involves all exchanges of goods, services or revenue. Products or services that generate revenue or are expected as part of a service are also included in the tangible value flow as are formal deliverables, such as contracts, proposals and invoices.

Intangible value consists of informal knowledge and support including strategic information, planning knowledge, process knowledge, technical know-how, collaborative design and policy development, which support the product and service-tangible value network.

Intangible benefits include favors that can be offered from one person to another. Examples include offering political or emotional support to someone. Another example of intangible value is when a research organization asks someone to volunteer time and expertise to a project in exchange for the intangible benefit of prestige by affiliation.

Sometimes value networks can be groups of companies working together to produce and transport a product to the customer. A good example is the partnership between Procter & Gamble and Wal-Mart. Customers can also create value networks—such as mothers who form a community on a baby care product site, like the Huggies Baby Network. Companies can create value through linking their customers together by direct methods like the telephone and website or indirect methods like combining customers' resources together for production or delivery.

The intangible value of knowledge within these networks is just as important as the monetary value of the product or service; it creates the best solutions or opportunities.

Understanding the transactional dynamics is vital for purposeful networks of all kinds, including networks and communities focused on creating knowledge value. A value network analysis helps communities of practice negotiate for resources and demonstrate their value to different groups within the organization. It is possible to develop scorecards, conduct ROI and cost/benefit analyses, and drive decision-making.

Because the value network approach addresses both financial and non-financial assets and exchanges, it expands metrics and indexes beyond the lagging indicators of financial return and operational performance to also include leading indicators for strategic capability and system optimization.

Verna Allee talked with us about how to establish high-performance value networks by implementing four propositions:

1. Visualize and organize the enterprise as a network, not an organization chart.

2. Make roles the building blocks of the network, replacing the concept of jobs.

3. Reward roles for creating value instead of compensating jobs for completing tasks.

4. Replace process thinking with relationship thinking.

VISUALIZE AND ORGANIZE THE ENTERPRISE AS A NETWORK, NOT AN ORGANIZATION CHART

In today's organizations, we are compelled to work with the starting point of the organization chart. It's all lines and boxes, and hierarchies, and reporting relationships, and vertical accountabilities and rigidities. It's a problem—a barrier to network thinking. The first instinct is to get rid of it. My earliest thinking was that value networks mean the end of the organization chart.

Gradually, however, I realized that the organization chart serves some very useful purposes. In its worst aspects, the organization chart is a destabilizer.

Organization charts are always getting changed around, creating confusion. The value network is the stabilizer in the organization. But the organization chart can still be useful as a resourcing tool for the new roles of people working with technology in a value network; its purpose should be rethought to support the necessary roles and interactions that create value.

MAKE ROLES THE BUILDING BLOCKS OF THE NETWORK, REPLACING THE CONCEPT OF JOBS

In a value network system, any one person might play three or four different roles in three or four key value networks in the organization. We don't know how to model that. We know how to model the organization chart, but we don't know how to model how the work gets done. We have started to model people talking with each other in communications networks inside and outside the enterprise, which produces a really good perspective to understand how people communicate and how knowledge flows, but it doesn't show us business transactions.

The value network is not simply about communication, it's about how communication converts knowledge assets into revenue and profit.

The first important step is to define the roles and interactions that make the system—the value-creating network. Once defined, it's important to avoid simply trying to import the definition into an organization chart. The way to avoid the organization chart lies in the idea of teams. Value networks are simply an expansion of the definition of a team. People understand teams. They can deal with the idea that teams can be very large. We can look at teams as networks and, when we're defining them, we can assign people on the team to play roles in those networks. We can assign people to those roles just as we assigned them to teams and special projects in the past. It isn't actually profoundly different but the fact that we can hold on to the old, while we are learning how to do something new, is reassuring to people. And reassurance is essential.

THE DIFFERENCE BETWEEN ROLES AND JOBS

Jobs are defined as a set of tasks to be completed. A task is a list of things that you do in your job; it is measured around events and outputs. The role is defined by what value it contributes. The organizational direction is: "Here's the role we want you to play; here's what we expect of that role; here are the value outputs required of that role; yet, how you play that role is up to you."

The evaluation question is: How effectively are you playing the role overall? We all have tasks that we do well and not so well. If I can't add, for example, I get somebody else to do it for me, but I can still play a role of analyst very well.

The role requires being savvy. Who are you going to name to help you do the tasks that need to be done? What will you be doing in this role? So, we should be focusing on roles and not just jobs.

WHAT IF THERE WERE NO MORE JOBS?

An individual may be located in the sales department on the organization chart as a tier-three sales manager. The enterprise can set a pay scale around that position. But, even today, individuals wear multiple hats in any job. That sales manager is going to play three roles: a customer relationship role, a forecasting role, and a production feedback role. They have a defined value contribution in each of those activities and that's what they're going to focus on. Our performance management systems must gradually come to manage how many different roles the individual can play and how effectively they play them, instead of what jobs they do.

To do so, it's necessary to change the HR system. HR writes clear job descriptions, specifying what experience is needed, and then the system tries to match candidates exactly with that job description.

If an individual would like to do that job, but does not quite have that experience, it is enormously difficult to get hired to do it. The HR people have put themselves into a box by defining each job as having a specific set of tasks and requiring specific sets of experience to fill that task. They really put the handcuffs on themselves as far as finding talent or working flexibly with the talent they have. Maybe they don't need a full-time business analyst. Maybe with the right job description, based on roles, you might have someone be a business analyst one day and a production performance manager the next.

What if we lived in a world where there were no jobs? How would the work get done? How would we find the talent we need? How would we manage the talent, if there were no jobs?

REWARD ROLES FOR CREATING VALUE INSTEAD OF COMPENSATING JOBS FOR COMPLETING TASKS

If your company or unit is growing quickly, you might have five people in a small unit that are playing three or four roles each. As you grow you might have more people playing these roles. You might have 20 people, each of them finding new roles all the time. Each role demands resources needed to support the role. Meanwhile, HR is focused on job descriptions. Roles mean it is a struggle how to write job descriptions these days. It's almost impossible, because you have a built in conflict where people tend to take on the roles they are most suited for—regardless of their job titles.

And what happens as we are playing three or four roles? We get evaluated and paid for one job! This happens in business units as well. For example, in the Customer Interaction Network for Cisco Systems (refer to Chapter Seven) the compensation system paid for the job of providing information for customers who ask questions of call centers. However, there are at least three other roles that call center employees play:

1. *A strategic role, because they know what's happening with the whole population of partners and customers;*

2. *An advisory role to production because they are the first to know what the customer's issues are;*

3. *A design role, linking people who are creating new products and services with the customer needs those new products and services must meet.*

So call center frontline employees play all these roles; it requires time; it requires resources; it requires mastery of technology to work with the information and manage it and share it. Top management must be able to understand the additional value creation and fund those roles, not just pay employees to provide answers to customer questions.

Unfortunately, in most cases, the enterprise is content to let these critical roles just happen incidentally and not encourage the real sources of value creation—which is the cultivation of the roles and relationships that create insights and innovation. This happens because managers are struggling with the old way of thinking about jobs and functions.

CREATE A REWARDS SYSTEM TO ENCOURAGE MULTIPLE ROLES

The individual's job itself is to define and manage all the multiple roles that they play. They should be evaluated for the roles that they play, not for executing a list of tasks. They might get evaluated for one role by one manager, but by another manager for another role. If the job is defined by its roles, then the employee can be evaluated by roles and should be rewarded for playing those roles.

REPLACE PROCESS THINKING WITH RELATIONSHIP THINKING

The value network view is a living system—the pattern of life itself is the network. Human society is always multi-faceted. We're the ones who've imposed the hierarchy of the organization chart. We're the ones who imposed the linear view of the process. Networks are a little bit closer to a more natural understanding of how life itself really works.

With process thinking, we were deliberately building a mechanistic system. It is a wonderful perspective. Look at what we were able to create with that view, with those mechanistic processes. Incredible! Now we're in a different kind of world where a lot of the outputs that we've created are not hard goods, but are experiences, they're services.

However, people perform work, process maps do not. People collaborate around knowledge. When we design a collaborative value network, it is really, truly moving to see that people are connected, and that we all have to do work together to understand and be successful. So, that kind of natural collaboration emerges out of really being seen and being appreciated for the roles we play.

People who are connected to each other through their roles view work much more personally than they do with a process view. This is about them, not about their processes. This is about them and their relationships. They can now work across silos, whether corporate silos, national silos or regional silos.

We can't make people trust each other. What we can negotiate about and deliver are the trusted behaviors and relationships that people are looking for. That's about sharing information, that's about sharing business contacts, that's about delivering the transparency of the sales activity. The value network can do that.

Summary

► Organizations are networks of people creating tangible value from intangibles like knowledge and relationships.

► Defining roles and value network analysis is replacing defining jobs and organization charts. The result is a measurable increase in both productivity and growth.

► People are more innovative and effective when they can improve their work processes based on networked roles and relationships.

CHAPTER FOUR
DEVELOPING ORGANIC ORGANIZATIONS

▶ How can organizations become living organisms?

▶ How can there be order without anyone giving orders?

▶ What does it mean to manage tasks not people?

▶ How does good work make good teams?

▶ Why is doing less doing more?

▶ Why is eliminating waste the fastest route to high productivity?

We need a new, co-evolutionary environment capable of handling simultaneous complex social, technical, and economic challenges... The grand challenge is to boost the collective IQ of organizations and society.

— Douglas Engelbart

Google, considered one of the most successful companies created in the last ten years, has pioneered the systematic capability to raise the collective intelligence of its workforce.

Jamie Dinkelacker, the Engineering Manager for Google Maps, suggests these propositions for future organizations:

Organizations are shifting from proto-military structures (generals at the back, giving orders, and troops at the front executing them) to organisms— living entities. They are information-processing entities; they are intelligent, and one day may even become sentient.

Google is one of the new breed of companies that is actually organic. At Google, everyone has a role, but hierarchy is minimal. Order can arise without anyone giving orders. Google is exceptionally adaptive, because it has remarkable information about both its environment and about its own capabilities. It uses its own information-processing tools and its own unique approach to managing "tasks not people" to operate an organic information processing organization. This is how value is created today.

Any company can do this, because all companies have access to Google tools and can adopt the Google way of processing information.

In other words, the "Bust The Silos" proposition of people collaborating around knowledge using process and tools is actually successfully implemented at Google. Revenue growth has been 50% a year between 2006 and 2008, doubling revenue from $10.6 billion to $21.8 billion.

Jamie Dinkelacker discussed some of the important, yet counterintuitive, elements of managing within an organic company, such as:

- ▶ Productivity is achieved in teams with purpose: Good work makes good teams

- ▶ Process achieves clarity

- ▶ Elimination of waste accelerates productivity growth

- ▶ Manage tasks not people

- ▶ Do less with more so more gets done

GOOD WORK MAKES GOOD TEAMS

Jamie's specific area of interest is in creating software that users value. From an organizational development viewpoint, this requires a very challenging adaptation: bridging the huge gap between the expert developer as an individual and the complicated organizational aspect of creating and releasing very complex software.

As he surveyed typical business management advice on addressing this challenge, he observed, *"Typically, there is all this emphasis on team building. Most of it is nonsense. There is a lot of hype about it, there is a market that*

Developing Organic Organizations 33

supports it, there is an awful lot of money that changes hands about it—the net result is marginal at best. Because many of the people proselytizing team development miss the fundamental issue, and that is: Teams are together for a purpose. And if that purpose is clear and worth achieving, then usually a good team will form and perform.

A group of people, who may have had many sharing and trusting experiences, do not necessarily become productive if what they are working on is ambiguous, self contradictory, or not of high value. In absence of clarity, chaos ensues. But I began noticing quite a while ago that you could gel a really strong team by a clearly defined project, one that they felt was worth doing, so that they believed they were of good use.

Clarity Means Being Sure that the Work to be Done is Highly Specific.

Giving the work worth means articulating the call to a higher purpose. And that higher purpose is the personalization of the mindset of service to other people – the people who will become the users of the software.

The two can be combined in the organic company, then the teams charged with this specific, high-purpose task can be left alone to get it done.

Let's use the example of a team writing software code for a travel site. Their purpose must be to please the user—to make the user's task easy and satisfying. "I want to be able to book a flight. I also want to be able to cancel a booking." Phrasing work in the terms of the actual users is one way to achieve both the right level of clarity and the sense of higher purpose.

Compare that to a mindset of "We will manufacture this software that will have the following specifications." Very different. Just providing specifications does not have the element of human engagement. It doesn't capture developers' hearts.

Process Clarity

In addition to clarity of task and clarity of purpose, there is the clarity of process. There are many elements of software engineering that have to do with the code gene. For example, what we are building has myriad parts to it, but when we step back from those myriad parts we have the following two or three things that are most important to do now. So rather than having this very large thing and a very large plan, a clear process helps us to decide, "Here is the clear thing that needs to be done next, then after that here is the next thing." Process clarity transforms a daunting, amorphous, unclear task into a straight-forward matter of executing through a specific list of specific things in the right order, one after the other.

In addition to process clarity, there must be an expectation of 100% completion with excellence. I am now thinking about an organization, not just one individual developer being illuminated by midnight pixels as he or she crafts a unique moment. Because we work today in a world of plans, schedules and releases—with marketing and product management—having to do all of the other things that organizational life brings, software developers need to know what "done" means. When the software is "done," we can move to release, marketing and monetization. There is no "almost done" or "nearly done." To me, done is binary: true/false. It keeps things simple.

One of the ways to ensure effective forward progress is to minimize "work in progress." Work in progress is waste. It's very familiar to those who are acquainted with the Japanese production system, particularly Toyota and Lean Manufacturing. There's a Japanese word, muda (MOO-DA) that roughly translates to "any wasted human effort that does not have a productive outcome." Look at work-in-progress, look at plans for things that aren't going to be built, look at features that aren't needed right now, look at status meetings about these things – all of those are muda. They're waste. Part of having good work is to minimize the amount of muda—to not have much work in progress and to be able to view things that are done as done. Not "almost done." Done!

If something is done, it means that conversations about it are now all in the past tense. If conversations about something are not in the past tense, it is not done. Simple rule.

ACCELERATE THE CREATION OF
VALUE BY ELIMINATING WASTE

Resource consumption in an organization equates to "value plus waste." Thus, one way to really increase the creation of value from the same resources is to minimize waste so that a higher percentage of resources are contributing to a valued output.

DEVELOPING ORGANIC ORGANIZATIONS 35

A leader for the idea of creating value by eliminating waste is Taiichi Ono, creator of the Toyota production system. The Japanese model uses the term muda as a definition of waste. Muda can be defects and low production, waiting, having inventory, any kind of over processing or manufacturing breakdowns. So one of the best ways to create value is to start as soon as possible at minimizing waste. The hardest part in minimizing waste—as anyone skilled in the practice will tell you—is, in fact, learning to see waste. Waste is hard to see because an awful lot of waste is ingrained into the way things are done: work in progress, excess inventory, things that are uneven causing an awful lot of adaptation, or one-off customizations.

People who don't understand software may demand that you build a specific feature. You build that feature, so that's a one-off. It's not going to be used by anyone else. It doesn't really generalize to the architecture. You now have a legacy code based on what was needed at one time and that becomes very fragile and expensive to maintain. A consulting company typically does all one-offs. Companies such as Yahoo or Google do not. We do services. And the customization is built into the system so the customer can customize or the system customizes based on the customer's usage, but you're not creating one-offs.

By focusing on waste, learning to see waste, making sure that processes can be smoothed out to remove waste, and ensuring that human beings are not overburdened by work are three unbelievably effective ways in any organization to improve the rate at which value can be created. Resources equal value plus waste. I believe these rules will apply wherever human minds are the key element of the value creating productive process.

What Toyota has done is astonishing: Focus on the work, not on the person. Toyota management shows a very deep respect for individuals. "Here is the work we have to do. You are professionals; you figure out how to do it. My job as a manager is to say, 'Here are our priorities,' not to micromanage." Managers in this environment manage tasks, not people.

MANAGE TASKS, NOT PEOPLE

Hands-on management is absolutely necessary in the organic organization. But it is very different from traditional American management.

The traditional management approach is constrained and debilitated by an industrial mass manufacturing mindset that uses human beings as the resource that you load "to a max level," as if they were machines.

This is wrong. Humans are interesting creatures; they are disorderly and they cannot be scheduled, predicted or treated as machines. Managers have been trained to try to manage people, rather than manage the work getting done. Now this is a subtle, but watershed, difference for having productive groups or teams. If a manager is worried about what Pat, John, Joe, Sally and Amir are doing, then everything becomes focused on those individuals. On the other hand, if the manager respects the work and focuses on the task, rather than the individuals who are doing the task, then he or she can make sure that the tasks are flowing as smoothly as possible. Now the naïve person will say, "Well, tasks are all done by people, so you have to focus on the people." No, Grasshopper, that's not the case. If the manager focuses on the work and not the people, then the people focus on the work, and not on themselves nor on each other. They are then able to partake in a purpose that is of a higher order.

So how would a manager communicate differently? The manager might say, "Given that we are doing tasks one and two, what's done? What's blocking us from getting these done?" Now, this isn't talking about what individuals are doing. The focus is on the elements of the task and what's blocking the task. So what will happen with a good group is that people will start to volunteer rather than wait to be assigned. Another typical probe question would be, "You are running at a particular level of traffic. What will it take for our software to scale to twice that? To ten times? Who wants to take on a test to learn that?" Focus on the work and ask for volunteers, rather than assigning tasks.

The naïve manager tends to misunderstand the human role. Here's what the naïve manager does. Five people may report to him or her. There are five tasks to do. The manager will assign each person a task. Now, that is counterproductive. My key observation over decades is that this is the root cause of many software project failures.

Let us begin with the obvious reason. First, if there is one individual working on a task, with the normal vagaries of human life, whether it is eldercare or childcare, going on vacation or getting a cold, having a dental appointment, or being interrupted by something perceived to be higher priority, that task does not slow down; it stalls. And if it is stalled, then it is work in progress—often with no progress at all. Work has a "half-life." When something stalls, it winds up becoming more

DEVELOPING ORGANIC ORGANIZATIONS 37

and more waste, especially in the world of software where it becomes progressively out-of-date. And the money put into it becomes an ever more squandered resource. This is waste at its worst.

Don't think in terms of having five people and five tasks, where it's one per person. Upgrade your thinking. If we have five tasks, how can we team on those five tasks to get the most important one done first?

Is that something for which we need two people? Do we need three or four people? Then focus on getting the most important task done first. Let's say that it takes three people. Well, two people can then work on the next most important task. The myth is that this is slower because you would have everyone working on all of these things simultaneously. The facts are quite different – by having no individual on a critical chain, we assure the work gets done (which is more important than whether Nick or Nora did it).

It's only in a perfect world that five people working on five tasks will all continue apace. It also misses one of the most fundamental points in software engineering. The majority of software development is new product development. These are things that have never been done before, or if they have been done before, have been done by a competitor and those are trade secrets. There is no book of "best practices" to look up and learn how to do something. People need each other for their mentality to bloom.

Because software is a complete fabrication of the human mind, it has perhaps an infinite and incalculable number of ways of doing anything. We know the human mind can tend to fixate. How we work is our mindset. Some people have different personality traits. Some people believe that the first idea they have is the only idea and they have to fight for it. Other people will not take any ideas; they blow through them. Social dynamics are a necessary condition in the development of software— particularly exciting, sometimes forbidding, ideas. Writing code can be extremely stressful. It is an arduous, detail-oriented skill. Few people have either the capability or the discipline to be an effective computer scientist or software engineer. It demands an excruciating attention to detail. Being so focused on little details does not necessarily lead to thinking about the big picture and broad-scale integration. So, conversation is essential for effective software development.

But if people are only having conversations about their own thing, then it is what psychologists call "parallel play." So go back to the naïve manager who has five tasks with five people with one assigned to each task. That's basically an organization engaged in parallel play. And we know from the literature on human development that's the play of a two-year-old toddler. So by doing this, the manager has driven a group of highly educated, highly skilled, highly disciplined people back to being two year olds. Everyone is working on his or her own thing. What do they have to talk to each other about other than lunch and whether or not they like their surroundings? In contrast, when several individuals are working together on the task that we set as a priority, then we have three people who have something in common to talk about. And in that common talking about things, they bring to bear their capabilities of big picture as well as their capabilities of being extremely focused and detail oriented. Collaboration enhances value creation.

That means there is less work underway at any one time. Hence, the phrase: "Do less with more (so more gets done)." Rather than having five tasks underway with five people, there are only two tasks underway with five people. This way, key things get done sooner. The tally of things that are actually "done" adds up. Then people move on to the next.

Consequently, this is where this hidden presumption of the industrial manager—the mass production manager – becomes apparent. He or she tends to use people as machines and thinks that the machines themselves have to be kept fully loaded. That's silly! We know wherever human performance is required that multiple humans are necessary. There's no stage show that does not have understudies for the lead roles. There is no firehouse that only has one person there. There is no emergency room that only has one attendant. Wherever human response is required, then humans are doubled up. Whether it is teaching, whether it is a court of law, there's always a backup. Yet, we get into the world of the corporation that is a total human artifice – the creation of organization software so to speak—and we act as if every person is for him or herself. We don't recognize that organizations are a complete artifice and that humans have to be interacting, not necessarily doing something that current management methods measure as "productivity."

THE FAILURE OF PRODUCTIVITY MEASURES

Most productivity metrics are flawed because they measure a person, rather than measuring what's done. A classic example in software is counting uncommented lines of code or number of feature points. Both lines of code and feature points are artifices that have come out of the industrial mindset of counting what a person does. Yet, software is highly intangible. Two people in a room for an hour at a white board aren't necessarily coming up with any lines of code. They may not even be working at all on feature points. In contrast, they may be talking about an algorithm. But there's no way to measure a discussion about an algorithm in the mass manufacturing mindset. Their new algorithm may be remarkable intellectual property and patentable. It might allow a service to speed up by some dramatic measure, to achieve a lower cost, or provide much better service. So the mass manufacturing mindset of trying to count what individuals do, as well as trying to load each developer with a large task list, is a method of management that while perhaps good for building cars or for packaging Twinkies, may not be helpful to the way software development works. Bankruptcy courts are littered with companies applying these outdated approaches to today's realities. To quote Einstein, "Not everything that can be counted counts, and not everything that counts can be counted."

DO LESS WITH MORE, SO MORE GETS DONE

Let's continue this notion of "do less with more." When a task is underway with more than one person, then that task itself does not stop. It may slow down if someone has eldercare, childcare, goes on vacation… but the focus here is on the task, not the individual. As a consequence, progress on the task continues. What I have noticed over the past 15 years is that managing software in this manner guarantees continual forward progress. And continual forward progress means that more software gets written, more tasks get completed. The traditional management mindset—what exactly did this person do versus what did that person do—hinders the value creation process. As soon as that starts happening, we're back to a group of individuals engaged in parallel play, and we're not a team. So an organization has to decide early on which of the following mutually exclusive choices is more important to them. Do they want to be a highly productive organization or do they want to keep track of all the individuals?

Keeping track, on a very granular level, of all the individuals and what all the individuals do: (a) uses a flawed measurement system that we know doesn't work; and, (b) leads everyone to naturally think that it's every person for him or herself.

On the other hand, an organization that is really productive focuses on getting the tasks done. It puts the load on the people, and consumes their time in getting the most important tasks done. If you have people on salary, if you have peer reviews, and you have the mechanisms that build strong teams, then people will want to be on winning teams. Slugs aren't invited to winning teams; no more than they are invited to be picked on a team for sandlot baseball. The more that someone performs excellently, the more that others want to draw them to their teams.

A LIVING EXAMPLE OF THE ORGANIC ORGANIZATION

At Google we live by our own tools. You don't see us sending PowerPoint presentations or many attachments back and forth. That's a highly wasteful (and costly) approach to operations. You see us using Google docs where anybody can edit. Google is a very open environment. Inside the company, everyone has a role and hierarchy is not a hindrance. Order can arise without anyone giving orders. And I believe that Google is an instance of an organization that has come to understand that a company is really an information-processing entity.

Rather than having a faux-military operation of the hierarchy with the generals and commanders and all the big strategies, rather than that whole industrial mindset or large mechanistic machine, Google is one of the new breed of companies that is actually organic. This is not a mechanistic environment; it is an organic environment. It is exceptionally adaptive. Now for a company to be exceptionally adaptive, that means it has to have remarkable information about both its environment and about its own capabilities.

History shows us that most companies don't adapt; they die. The bankruptcy courts all around us are trumpeting the failure of the industrial-mechanical mindset of corporate governance. Any company can use the same tools we do. Look at tools like Google Trends, Google Suggest, Google Docs, Gmail, Google Alerts, and so on, and all the ways that these tools are part of the Google offering. We have figured out how to use those in order to enhance the productivity of our people. This is what "the cloud" promises to all organizations.

Summary

- ▶ Eliminate waste

- ▶ Focus on tasks, not people

- ▶ Structure work around teams and not individual projects

- ▶ Build organic, not mechanistic organizations

CHAPTER FIVE
TRANSFORMING FROM SALES AND MARKETING TO DEMAND CREATION

▶ What skills sets are now necessary for Sales Management?

▶ How can technology level the sales service playing field?

▶ How to better help the customers achieve their own objectives?

▶ How to train to be able to deliver on the company value proposition?

▶ What makes the Demand Creation role so fascinating?

Integration is not something you do and move on. It has to be continuous; it takes a long time; and it forces the whole organization to change. And, basically, functional specialists don't like change.

— Don Schultz

Let us introduce Mark Ouyang. He represents an atypical, but perhaps growing new breed of sales professional. In his career, Mark has been a direct sales rep, sales trainer, partner manager, program manager, and customer success manager. He has worked at large companies – Xerox, McDonnell Douglas, EDS – mid-sized companies – Network General, Netscape, Documentum, NetManage – and small startups-Analog Design Tools, Everdream and Clickability. The constant is that every company he has worked for has been "high-tech." Mark has a veteran's perspective in how technology and advances in today's web platforms have transformed customer service and made "Internet Time" a reality everywhere. He provides a forward view of where Demand Creation is today and where it may go from here.

Integration of Sales, Marketing, and IT

What has really changed with the advancement and adoption of technology is speed. Everyone is now operating on "Internet Time." Not only do you have to respond faster, but better. You must integrate what had previously been "silos of information." A real boon to satisfying customer needs is access to better, instantaneous customer information—just simple contact information and customer preferences are now available on systems. More than just automated sales forecasting or customer acquisition processes, you can now coordinate systems among lead generation, Demand Creation, sales force automation, and support. Customers' overall expectations have a greater likelihood of being fulfilled in the engagement and product delivery process.

The Evolution of the Sales Job—Getting the Company to Deliver on the Value Proposition

I began my career working as a rep for Xerox to establish my sales credentials. Back then there was greater emphasis on motivating the sales rep. A Sales Manager's primary role was to make sure the rep survived the wear-and-tear of simply going through the rejection process multiple times before getting a sale; to make sure that they knew the product, knew the current promotions, and just getting them out there.

But now, Sales Managers need different skill sets: being able to work with a software program like SalesForce.com, obtaining and generating their own reports, and doing queries and "what if" type questions. Those are the new requirements of a Sales Manager—in addition to being a good salesperson, in addition to knowing the product or the service, in addition to familiarity with the internal operations of the company. Getting the customer to sign the order is the easy part; now, it's getting the order through the system and getting the company to deliver on the value proposition—that is the hardest part of the job!

Is There More Functional Integration?

Yes and no. If you are using a system like SalesForce.com, which has customer support modules as well as integration with marketing campaigns and lead generation efforts, then the manager can integrate functions. But you have to be comfortable with the complexity of the software and know where to look. You have to know how to use the reporting query features.

ALIGNMENT OF SALES AND MARKETING DEPARTMENTS

You would think that the sales and marketing groups, at least upstream in the acquisition process, would be closely aligned. But that isn't always the case. Often you hear salespeople complain about marketing and vice versa. My explanation for the carping is due to operating in different "time" perspectives.

Sales is definitely focused on the here-and-now—more on a daily or weekly time horizon – while marketing has to plan a little bit further ahead. Marketing plans on a quarterly basis for media venues, events, cooperative partnerships, and the other types of periodical messaging with PR and Advertising Agencies. So there's always a tendency for the salespeople, because of their immediate focus on revenues, to say, "Those marketers, what are they doing? They're just in the clouds." And I think that has more to do with their immediate time perspective (What can you do for me today?) because tomorrow is a totally different day. It's hard to even imagine how fast the business changes—even hourly.

GOOD INFORMATION AND TIMING CAN MEAN EVERYTHING

When you have information literally at your fingertips, you can be more productive at a much faster pace. If you didn't systematically record each piece of contact information – mobile phone, land line, and fax number – then you would be spending more time searching for that information than it takes to make the call.

Suppose you want to do a quick account review, but you really haven't talked to that account for a couple of months. You want to know what's happening "at the moment." With an integrated CRM system, like SalesForce.com, you can look into a customer's current technical support cases and check what is going on. Because your client support organization has more frequent, day-to-day operational contact with your customer, you would be able to leverage their work. You could see if there are any outstanding cases and what are potential issues you should be prepared to address. Usually, those matters are well documented. You would anticipate the reception or tone that you might receive from the customer. That is all without having to talk to anyone in your client support group. If they kept the information up-to-date in the system, then you could see that for yourself. You could see the account history, you could see how problems have or have not been resolved. Is now a good time to do an account review? Maybe you need to be spending more time internally with the organization and making sure that those issues are resolved before you ask the customer for a favor or ask him or her to be a reference. Good information and timing can mean everything.

SALES SYSTEMS CAN LEVEL THE PLAYING FIELD

The majority of SalesForce.com users are very small businesses in comparison with companies like GE and P&G; the reality is that technology levels the playing field. Companies with fewer than 2000 employees now can have systems that would have been previously out of reach to small businesses. They can provide the same sophistication in customer programs and satisfaction as larger companies, yet they still maintain their nimble flexibility to respond to changing customer and competitive circumstances.

Successful smaller companies recognize that the customer is the focus of their business. They need to make the technology work for them just in meeting expectations and following up on their own commitments. I have so many daily transactions and am disciplined about putting those into the system. Using the notes section, I record the conversation or commitments. I can see that a few weeks ago we had this discussion, these were the action items, and here's how we are proceeding.

Technology systems also help when you have turnover in a company. The era of working 30 years at one company is long gone. Today, before the age of 36, a person might have had 10 jobs. New workers are coming into the work force and the corporate or account history should be transferred. If the information is there, you can provide a consistency that helps keep the customer relationship at a very high satisfaction level.

One reason for the downfall of Xerox Corporation was because they had so much quick turnover: every six months! I remember introducing myself as the new Xerox sales rep. And the person at the other end had gone through so many sales reps in the past two years, she said, "Yeah, how long are you going to be in this territory?" And she just kind of tossed my card to the side, because she had gone through that burnout of constant sales rep replacement. In that situation there wasn't an information handoff or relay between different reps, simply because they didn't have systems in place to convey or store that information.

CHANGE TO REAL TIME

The character of salespeople has not changed. They still need to have the drive, the focus to do that job. And the skills sets are challenging. But for most young people, using computers and technology is just a natural extension of what they have grown up with. Look at smart phones that were not even prevalent five years ago. Now there is integration between Blackberries and iPhones to MS Outlook and Salesforce.com. It's just the natural progression of things getting faster, more accurate and more " real time." John Naisbitt wrote the book, <u>Megatrends: Ten New Directions Transforming Our Lives</u>, way back in 1985. Some of those trends are still playing themselves out. One was this change from a periodic timeframe to a real-time timeframe. For example, gas prices used to be very stable, and with the change in markets, gas prices are more volatile and change day-to-day like the stock market does. The prediction that in real time, every minute, the price of gasoline will change, like the price of stocks will change, has come to fruition.

IT TAKES A WHOLE COMPANY TO FULFILL
THE VALUE PROPOSITION

Markets now change so quickly. Consider the appearance of YouTube in February 2005. Before then, it wasn't even on the radar screen; no one could have predicted it. And now, it's just assumed that video is a part of our lives on the Internet. So the value proposition that you deliver to businesses can radically change. You just have to be open to anything. We have customers who are trying to manage their online presence with web technology that they develop. We learn from our customers what they want to do with their ideas, making sure that the technology and framework we provide can accommodate them. So any salesperson, whether it's pre-sales or post-sales, just has to be on top of that kind of stuff. And they have to be able to ask good questions. We need to be adaptable to their business context, understand what our customers are trying to do, and then figure how the technology can help them to achieve it. We are interdependent in helping achieve the value proposition. You know the old saying, "It takes a village to raise a child." Well, it takes a whole company to fulfill the value proposition.

Everyone Works for Marketing

We have another saying here, "Everyone works for marketing." The brand that you promote, that you have an image out there or expectation that customers expect to be fulfilled.

Fulfilling customer satisfaction starts very early. Before you even have contact, there is some understanding or image about your company's brand. And then what you can actually deliver is limited by skill set, experience, and money. The point is that you'll have a customer satisfaction gap if that expectation is way above what you can actually deliver. You can be perceived as underperforming even if what you do is 100% right on and you didn't mess up on anything. Make sure there is no gap between the expectations and the actual delivery of the product or service. If you over promise in the marketing, no matter what, you will still have a problem.

In our company we are very careful to make sure we do not over promise ("Here's what we can do, here's the expectation.") because we know that our customers on the line have a boss or have a set of stakeholders they have to get back to and they have to manage their expectations. So everything is really focused on making sure the expectation and the delivery of the eventual service or product is aligned. There is a whole process from the first encounter on our website all the way to signing the contract.

How to Manage With Constant Change

Companies have to focus on change as a constant rather than as an episode. Realize the on-boarding process of bringing someone in is much more compressed. I'll give you an example. When I started in sales at Xerox, it was basically six months in training before you even got into a territory or were given the responsibilities of dealing with a customer. Six months! Nobody has that luxury anymore. Sales people are onboard and, within two weeks, they are thrown in to sink or swim. If they're fortunate, they have a new-hire sales training program. Basically, many companies invest in training only their salespeople. Why? Because they generate revenue! Everyone else, you're kind of on your own. Figure it out! Read the website! You know, good luck!

Some large companies will realize the value of a new-hire orientation program. But those are usually more established, well-rounded, stable companies.

What frequently happens over time is that non-sales personnel get invited to the program. I have had my new-hire sales training program in one of my companies that had 80 people in it. And how did I get 80 people? They weren't hiring 80 salespeople. What they said was, "This is the only new-hire orientation available. It's for the sales force, but can you please add on these new marketing people and add these people that are coming in from HR and Finance?"

When that happens, the quality of that program suffers. How can one instructor manage 80 people in the class? It is just untenable. But on the other hand, I recognized that it was the only program that would orient people to their new employer. And company management eventually realized that there was value in carving out some of that program for new hires that were not sales oriented.

HOW TO TRAIN TO DELIVER ON THE COMPANY VALUE PROPOSITION

It's ridiculous to think that anyone could learn everything they needed to know even in a week of training.

The sales rep's attention span drops off dramatically after two days. And to make them go through a training program over a week is really asking a lot. At Netscape our sales orientation lasted two weeks because that's how comprehensive the product line was. Knowing that, if you wanted to keep their enthusiasm, as well as what they need to know and do, the only thing you could realistically teach them in two days was the framework. My goal was to teach them the questions they should ask. Then have continuing education when they were in the field with their managers, their peers, and the systems that were available. This way, they could learn by doing or learn to answer questions when they're most motivated to learn, which was typically when a customer or their manager was asking them some question that they needed to provide a quick answer to.

That's the ideal situation; it barely ever works out that way, but you do the best you can. That's one of the challenges I think about when you come up with training programs. You know you have so much to convey, but how to tell the story over a period of time when their motivation to learn and absorb is at its highest. There's always been a mismatch.

(Chapter Six on Genentech illustrates this principle of informal learning as the core value in a learning organization)

SOLVING PROBLEMS IS AT THE HEART OF THE DEMAND CREATION (SALES) ROLE

I appreciate this role by approaching it as "solving problems." At the heart of what people are asking for when they are looking for a product or service is to solve a problem. I am fascinated by just going through that whole understanding process of what challenges they face and matching what the product or service can do for them. The whole image of the sales profession in the media, movies and television is typically negative. Think of the image created by "Death of a Salesman," "Tin Men", "Cadillac Man," "Glengarry Glen Ross" and you know what I mean. Yet, when you also think about it, the people who make it to the top, the captains of our industries, the CEOs of our large corporations are usually salespeople. Because that's where the rubber meets the road; when you actually meet with customers, get into all the specific nuances, negotiations, and the delicate dance of building rapport. Those skill sets are all very hard; you cannot just teach them. You acquire them based on your personality, character and unique professional experiences. It is also fascinating to see how different people handle those situations in different ways; yet see how each of them can still be very successful in that role.

Summary

▶ Requirements have changed in the transformation of the Sales Management function to Demand Creation.

▶ Business process combined with technology is a great advantage for Demand Creation.

▶ Successful integration of functions is important to be customer centric: everyone works for marketing.

Part Two: The Transforming Power of the Active Organization

CHAPTER SIX
HOW THE ACTIVE ORGANIZATION LEARNS—GENENTECH

▶ What are the guiding principles for a dynamic learning organization?

▶ How does the Value Network become operational in a learning organization?

▶ How can marketing, sales, and IT become seamlessly integrated to serve the customer?

▶ How can new technologies be responsive for formal and informal highly specialized training?

Effective teaching may be the hardest job there is.

— William Glasser

Genentech is one of the leading biotech companies, with multiple products on the market for serious or life-threatening medical conditions. It is the market leader in anti-tumor therapeutics—fighting cancer and other unmet medical needs in Immunology, Lytics, and other disease states. There are few companies in any industry that can match Genentech for continuous product innovation. It is also innovative in the way it trains and develops its people.

Genentech has been ranked among the top employers in biotechnology and related industries six years running by *Science* magazine based on its commitment to innovative thinking. In 2008, FORTUNE again named Genentech to its annual list of the top 100 companies to work for—for the 10th consecutive year. Clearly, this is a company that knows how to create a value network through development of its human capital.

We chose Genentech to illustrate best practices in what can be considered a world class learning organization.

52   BUST THE SILOS

Becoming a Genentech salesperson may be one of the most challenging of sales positions. Salespersons are considered Clinical Specialists with a focus on consultative selling. The company is a leader in all areas of the drug development process—from research and development to manufacturing and commercialization. The technical, scientific, and legal requirements are daunting. So we spoke with Harry Wittenberg, who is responsible for integrating the development and delivery of sales training programs through the use of technology in coordination with the Genentech marketing and IT professionals, to serve the fast-growing Genentech sales force.

Harry Wittenberg was the Senior Manager for Learning Technologies for Commercial Training and Development for Genentech at the time this chapter was written. Any kind of electronically delivered learning experience comes through his five-person group: website development, portal development, online assessments, online learning, virtual classrooms, web conference classes, synchronized remote distance learning, and pod casts.

They design with their users (the sales force); work with IT for infrastructure; work with outside vendors who actually build out some of the content and help them maintain it; and they may get involved with end user support.

Here is Harry's perspective on making a learning organization operational.

HOW TO BEGIN

Anticipating that there would be major growth, I began with an extensive diagnostic study. I wanted to understand the existing challenges for current employees because I believed those challenges would exist for anyone new. So I actually worked with a group of knowledge architects to help me create a taxonomy of what information a salesperson would need and we did an extensive knowledge mapping session to really understand:

▶ *What are the content areas they need to know?*

▶ *Where are they finding it now, what's missing for them, what barriers do they have to get that knowledge?*

HOW THE ACTIVE ORGANIZATION LEARNS—GENENTECH 53

▶ *How much time are they spending looking for it?*

▶ *How often do they need it?*

▶ *From whom do they get information?*

▶ *Who do they need to deliver information to?*

From this Harry developed five key learning foundational guideposts that have focused his work.

1. One stop shopping: the learning portal as one place for all to access educational content.

   Field reps want one place to find all of the applications, information, and training content they need. It has to be easy, quick, and trustworthy.

   Their time is spent building relationships with their customers, not being online. For the little time they are online, they need to get information fast.

   Solution: a learning portal that contains content in one place, a structured learning plan and online resources such as eLearning modules, podcasts, and slide decks.

2. Teach me where you can find me: anytime, anyplace, and any venue.

   Field reps are required to be out in the field as much as possible. Trainers are beginning to rely more and more on learning events that won't take reps out of the field.

   Solutions: Virtual Classrooms are a combination of web conferencing and teleconferencing where a trainer or subject matter expert conducts a live learning session to a large or small group of learners synchronously. Reps dial in and access the visual content (usually slides) from their laptops at home or on the road.

Mobile learning delivery channels such as podcasting are utilized by deploying iPods to the field with a mechanism for delivering content seamlessly and effortlessly. This has proven to be very successful. Reps can listen to audio content in the car, and video content during short downtimes at the airport or in a doctor's waiting room. And based on legal requirements, some customer-facing content was made available for reps to train their customers—creating added value.

Content includes key messaging or reinforcement, marketing content, and archived recordings of virtual classrooms.

3. Keep me up to date on the latest scientific advancements and medical education.

Field reps want timely, in-depth knowledge to build fluency with customers and a focus on the details. They want it short and targeted, so they can understand the content quickly.

Solution: Informal learning "virtualizing" access through an online Journal Club to the most current journals relevant to their brand and providing them a means to ask questions on those articles to in-house science experts who can provide scientifically relevant answers to their questions in a "safe haven" environment.

4. Give me feedback.

Field reps (as adult learners) want to know how well they are learning.

Solution: Institute online assessments for knowledge checking at regular intervals (after each module) during home study. Use an online assessment tool for reporting in the home office and providing detailed reports on learner progress to the trainers.

In addition, the training organization also developed a sales training program that involved better coaching and feedback by managers for their reps using the results of the assessments.

HOW THE ACTIVE ORGANIZATION LEARNS—GENENTECH 55

5. Connect me to the experts.

> Field reps are asked questions by their customers that sometimes find them struggling to produce the right answers, especially in sales environments that are complex, such as biotech. They want access to experts who can provide them the best answers in the context of their work and within compliance regulations.

> Solution: Conduct regular virtual classrooms so live questions can be posed to the experts, and institute a virtual and online Journal Club where questions can be posted to the science experts in a compliant web environment.

Harry's group can then build scalable solutions to meet these needs. They have developed an assessment server to give the salespeople feedback to know how well they are learning. The Learning Technologies Group also instituted podcasting and started the online Journal Club.

In the five years Harry has worked at Genentech, the company has increased from 3,500 to 11,000 people, more than doubling its sales force.

Each new product launch comes with between 100–200 new salespeople who need training. They are trained as a cohort, as well as some of the sales forces of partner organizations that co-develop or co-sell a drug.

This is a challenge because Genentech maintains separate online services just for partners to keep them out of the company firewall.

Working with IT, Harry developed an external portal access point that limits partners to just areas in the Genentech network for training and they can go nowhere else. So, they can get everything they need for their training as if they were internal employees, but tunneled into a specific area. This saved a large expense just by providing the external access in one site rather than building and maintaining a special partner site hosted by an external vendor.

The Value of Ongoing Informal Education
Delivered through Technology

Our people who have already been trained need us even more once they are out in the field. The value of formal education is high when they are new. As the new reps' experience grows and their confidence builds, formal education isn't as much of an imperative. However, the informal access to information, experts and best practices through mobile learning becomes more important, because it's much more targeted and it supports activities that they're doing as they are making decisions and answering questions.

New hires spend the first four weeks almost full time in training. After that the amount of time spent specifically for learning diminishes greatly because they're meeting with customers.

Genentech has increased that learning time by making learning mobile through the iPods they have distributed to all the sales reps in the field. A Podcasting site through iTunes delivers content directly to them and sales reps have the opportunity to listen in their cars, waiting rooms, waiting for a flight, or anywhere they have a little downtime.

Marketing, IT and Sales Can Integrate
in a Selling Program

The Commercial Training and Development Group developed a customized selling excellence program with a lot of collaborative input from the marketing and sales functions. The language and the concepts of the selling excellence program are embedded in the marketing materials. So, now there is a more seamless flow and integration from marketing through sales using the same approaches and language: the right message is communicated; the right training is delivered and reinforced; the right behaviors are practiced; and the right customer interactions are maintained. Marketing is actually supporting the training that sales management has also contributed to. There is integration in language, approach, and messaging.

How the Active Organization Learns—Genentech 57

The sales reps are trying to get the customer from one level of performance to another in terms of prescription rates, or other metrics. That language is now coming into marketing and sales materials, and the key behaviors are showing up on field contact reports, where the salespeople are being assessed. Marketing and sales are now using the same vocabulary and concepts. So here the learning organization has had an impact in beginning to bridge the traditional gap between sales and marketing communication.

When it comes to technology, there was little web delivered learning. Much of it was just for new hires for a short period of time. Yet, at one time, Genentech was not really delivering the learning potential in assessment, feedback, and metrics as they do now.

Also, Genentech learning innovation had existed, but it was provided piece-by-piece or franchise-by-franchise (silos). Now everybody in all franchises gets this simultaneously. Harry's challenge is that sometimes it takes a while to come up with an idea, then present it to management, who has to back it, fund it, and then give him the time to work with IT to develop it.

Harry often proposes new learning applications that management might have never seen before. They need to get a full understanding of how it works, why it will add value, what the user will do with it and how it will be supported and maintained.

IT is brought in at the very beginning, right at the onset when a new idea is being proposed, for example, a learning assessment server. Harry is careful to align a learning technology solution with a business problem. Through needs assessment and observation, an idea for a new solution is generally introduced to one brand first. With backing from management, Harry engages with the IT group and demonstrates to management, "We know this assessment server is something that is important to us. Here is why we're doing it and this is where we think we can put it." This way IT can engage in the development and it makes them complete partners from the very beginning.

58   BUST THE SILOS

Harry concedes it may take more initial work to involve both IT and management early on, but this approach pays off in creation of a value network.

It's a challenge for IT to understand our business, to understand what we want to do, how we are going to build out the infrastructure, how we are going to support this. We mitigate that challenge by partnering with them at the very onset. Once we get management approval, then we work with IT to put it in, pilot it. We introduce it to one of the franchises through one of the managers who I know may be open to this innovation. We ask, 'How do you think your guys in the field are going to use this? How should we represent and introduce this?'

We worked with the franchises to really get them to understand what we wanted to accomplish, so they could embrace and implement it, which is usually the biggest challenge. How do you get people to use new and different learning tools and materials? They may see it as adding more time to their jobs rather than seeing the value it will bring later on. Learning is a process that takes time to realize the benefits—but when they do, they embrace these new capabilities for learning continuously and informally rather than just event-driven.

THE CHALLENGE OF A KNOWLEDGE-BASED SALES FORCE

Genentech's customers are specialists and physicians in certain disease states, such as different cancer tumors. So the sales force needs to understand the science, the physiology, the biology behind the disease state and be fluent. To establish credibility with a physician, the salesperson needs to get on their level for their disease state. There is a lot of knowledge to be mastered for salespeople to converse fluently with their customers.

A level above that is to understand what the company compliance strategy is, so that salespeople keep within the legal limit of a quite complex set of regulations.

And then above that is a strategy and protocol to assist the salesperson, who needs reinforcement about an issue immediately, to quickly access the resources to respond to the physician properly in order to get their questions answered.

HOW THE ACTIVE ORGANIZATION LEARNS—GENENTECH   59

Quite a lot to learn!

Harry has mapped different learning technology interventions to each of these levels.

A new hire will spend the first four-to-six weeks in foundation training in order to get the basics: understanding terminology, recalling facts, being able to just apply conceptual knowledge and build examples.

We have a very prescriptive curriculum that we present: an orientation of the basics that people need to know about the company, about their jobs and about benefits, etc. Moving up is foundation training—done remotely at home—which consists mostly of the core and critical knowledge, terminology, basic understanding of the science, terms, vocabulary and how everything fits in with the Genentech businesses.

Higher up on the pyramid is Core training to build fluency, apply concepts and build selling skills. A significant part of the time, they role-play in order to apply what they learned.

They are meeting customers, they are learning how to build on what they have learned. They can take the conceptual information and vocabulary that they developed and begin to build their messaging skills and influence.

Then when they're out in the field, that's when they begin to figure out the rules. And when they are out in the field for a while, they are presented with Advanced training where we continue to reinforce their fluency and build on all the concepts that they developed during Foundation and Core. It moves them from just applying knowledge to the level of creative thinking, of compare and contrast. At this point, they just need structured information to be able to strategize and make decisions.

For each one of those levels, Harry really needs to target that knowledge base and then create content that dynamically serves the salesperson.

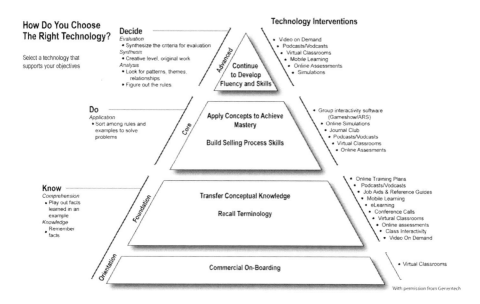

Figure 6-1 How Do You Choose the Right Technology?

How to Make the Experts and the Information Readily Available

Journal clubs are a useful informal learning venue in the biotech/pharma industry. But they can be unreliable if reps' questions cannot be answered when it comes to the science or the results of a clinical trial. So Harry developed an online version of the Journal Club to connect reps with Genentech's science experts. This is when real learning takes place.

Sales reps can't take a lot of time out of the field to attend formal training. But they can read an article when they have some downtime. And when they get the chance to get on the network, they can post a question. They know it will come back answered and they can see other questions that other salespeople ask that are also answered. Because it is archived, there is a continuously building knowledge repository that is always available whenever they need it.

Learning becomes really high value when it is very targeted at a high level with continuous access to experts who will give answers when needed. That is where Harry is concentrating his efforts.

Through podcasts and mobile technologies, salespeople will be able to access those key questions and answers when they need it. That provides high impact for the organization.

Another application for distance learning is in response to reps that needed a safe practice environment to engage in dialogue with their customers. Harry went a step further and built a decision tree simulation using an algorithm developed by the Marketing group. Sales reps can see and model a conversation based on their choices. Depending on the choices the rep makes, the program presents a more specific situation and gives advice on how to respond to it.

This is a high-value learning experience, because sales reps saying those words, as they would in a real sales call, is better than just reading from a piece of paper – which is good for reinforcement, but does not do the job for modeling behavior.

How to Make It Work Across All
Product Lines

I believe you have to look at the entire learning spectrum and the whole ecology of the way the audience lives. I think having a curriculum structure that can be translated across different business lines is crucial, because, as a training organization, we don't want to custom build curriculum structures for every product franchise. It costs too much; you can't be responsive enough; and the usability, or the reusability, becomes difficult. So, if there's a way that you can create a basic curriculum structure that can be applied across business units, then you can deliver more product and audience relevant content with less effort. The other thing is to keep learning theory right in your line of sight.

People who came from sales and marketing departments sometime in their careers get to run training organizations. Because of where they came from, it is natural for them to focus on numbers rather than looking at content and not approach or instructional design. The result is: more is better, which is not always true. Keep the instructional design of how people learn, how people interact with information, and how technology can deliver that content in the process. We have figured out all of these things pretty well.

Every technology Harry has introduced is completely integrated with the curriculum and supported by the business.

Its effectiveness has been in the ability to get the right learning to the right person at the right time, providing feedback to reps learning new material, and providing management with the metrics to show effectiveness and return on investment.

To make it even more convenient for reps to learn on the go, whenever there was downtime, Harry recently added a new addition to the learning

HOW THE ACTIVE ORGANIZATION LEARNS—GENENTECH   63

technology infrastructure. It was a capability that did not even require the time to open a laptop – podcasting.

But for new innovations to get support from management, they have to be designed not only for the convenience and effectiveness of the learner, but, just as importantly, to the budget and resource allocations to support it. One example is a podcasting infrastructure that is a turnkey solution involving multiple vendors. Essentially, new audio or video content is developed, then delivered to the vendor for a complete packaging and uploading to the website.

When new podcasting content is ready, all we do is send the vendor an email saying, 'I have a new podcast for you, pick it up on the network and deliver on a certain date. You take care of it; you put it into the correct format, include the necessary disclaimers to put on the website; and update the webpage. Just tell us when you're done.' And so now we can scale because we have outside vendors who can completely do this for us; we can concentrate on innovation and other things that are much more difficult or really require our unique skill set.

Another project underway is the streamlining of the development process and delivery and tracking of training materials. The Commercial Learning Management Solutions project is designed to deliver an integrated solution for ongoing training and support that can be applied to any size of sales force no matter how many new drugs come online.

The Future Integrated Solution Figure illustrates the system.

64 BUST THE SILOS

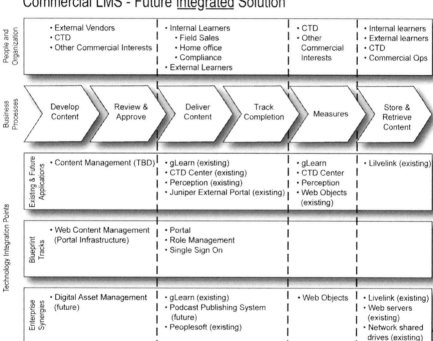

Figure 6-2 Future Integrated Solution

TECHNOLOGY IS LEVERAGED IN THE GENENTECH CULTURE

Harry discusses how the technology should fit the needs of the business and its learners.

They need a very simple interface, because they are extroverted; they are impatient; they are salespeople; they are very personable and think the same qualities should apply to the program. You need to be smart; you need to be quick; you need to be personable; you need to be able to relate to your customers very well; and you need to be able to learn very quickly, because things do change fairly rapidly.

It is telling that our CEO says we are a technology company. Of course, we are a biotechnology company, but in the sense that we use technology to our advantage. Whether it is to create new molecules or manufacturing drugs or training our sales force, we try and leverage technology. So that's been a focus. Of course, if people that we bring in aren't tech savvy, we hope they become comfortable with technology, because we employ a lot of it.

While there are no exact metrics for what it costs to train each salesperson at Genentech, there are several clear benefits that management believes have added great value to the Genentech market advantage through the Commercial Training and Development program that Harry has supported with technology:

- ▶ Bringing cost efficiency by being able to apply technology creatively and effectively

- ▶ Upgrading the quality of education that people get so they are proficient when they "hit the ground"

- ▶ Aligning technology solutions to the needs of the business

- ▶ Instituting online assessments to make sure learning was happening.

FIT IS CRUCIAL

People today are looking for their fit within the organizational culture. Genentech has always prided itself on being a very open culture, where people are valued for their ideas, their intelligence, and for their ability to influence others, because that's how things happen. Here you can't just wait to be told to do something. We like people who know what they want to do, sell it, and get support for it. I think the people who gravitate to this company, who have come from larger pharmaceuticals, are looking for that—a medium-sized place or company that has its passion behind it. One thing about Genentech: people here have passion for innovation and that permeates throughout everyone's work, everyday.

THE FUTURE IS IN INFORMAL LEARNING

I think business education will lean more toward informal, on the job learning, which is where 80% of learning happens anyway for most people. There is a lot of trial and error; time wasted trying to get to the right answer. They eventually get it, but they have expended quite a bit of energy to get there. Better knowledge architecture of content is needed, so people can browse and find things more quickly. I think we will be developing better search engines, so the appropriate information gets rated higher.

Informal learning does not have to be structured. You don't have to be in a structured environment to learn something new, so a podcast is a venue for that kind of informal learning. We can present some information and make it available to the folks in the field, and when they need it, give them a way to go in and search to find what they need quickly.

Also the building of social networks, where they can have access to people that they need to get expert advice from when they need it. I see mobile technology come into play.

Medium and larger companies are using technology to train their sales forces and get them productive more quickly and effectively. If you are just going to be using book knowledge, you are missing out. You need to provide the opportunity to apply learning—basically, applying the knowledge more often as opposed to reading a

HOW THE ACTIVE ORGANIZATION LEARNS—GENENTECH 67

body of theory and knowledge and then applying it. I think that this incremental application on demand—tied in with the opportunity for social networking and access to the experts—is the answer. Expand the expert base and through curiosity and their own need to know, individuals begin to figure out how to find inside resources; this is the future. The best people do it all the time. If they need an answer, they go and try to find it.

BUILDING THE COLLECTIVE INTELLIGENCE OF THE ORGANIZATION

Just as Verna Allee (Chapter 3) believes value networks are the foundations of successful companies, Harry Wittenberg believes raising the collective intelligence of the organization through structured social networks brings a competitive edge and agility with a big pay off.

It goes back to knowledge management. This is the Holy Grail for a lot of places, because it's not a very easy thing to do. It is labor intensive to capture knowledge; it's hard to extract passive knowledge from somebody and place it in a structured format for it to be used at the time of need by a learner. New social networks of knowing and changing peoples' roles will be evolving. If they are viewed as experts, then that becomes part of their job. It should not be, if I have time I will help you. Rather, if you need help, part of my job is to make time to help you.

Harry Wittenberg's experience at Genentech provides a good example of how innovation, through the smart use of technology and instructional design, can accelerate learning effectiveness.

Summary

- ▶ Technology, instructional design, and structured knowledge have the potential to transform the organizational culture and capacity to learn as never before.

- ▶ Informal learning on demand is the most important innovation in training and development—it is possible to deliver learning "in the work" and scale it for medium and large organizations.

- Social networking and value networks are greatly enhanced through ongoing learning and development.

- Marketing, sales and IT can integrate seamlessly when brought together at the onset of training and development programs.

Chapter Seven
How the Active Organization Creates
New Value via Global Customer Service — Cisco

▶ Why is being adaptive necessary for organizational survival?

▶ How to design a customer support system that listens and teaches rather than just fix problems?

▶ How to take full advantage of the web for customer support?

▶ How to give the front-line professionals the training and tools to be consultants rather than mechanistic problem solvers?

▶ How can evolving metrics be a game changer?

An enterprise's purpose begins on the outside with the customer... it is the customer who determines what a business is, what it produces, and whether it will prosper.

—Peter Drucker

We all now operate in a highly connected, rapidly evolving, customer-centric and knowledge-driven environment. Yet, most of our current management practices, organizational models and job functions are not effective in serving our customers.

Value is created through relationships with customers. Companies must adopt principles and practices that encourage every individual in their diverse groups of employees to have a shared sense of purpose to engage in more effective ways of working together to build customer intimacy and loyalty.

The Service Paradox

Customers value relationships over efficiency, yet service and support organizations are driven by efficiency. Furthermore, while customer service and support systems are usually constructed around predictability (think about FAQs), business problems – particularly those with complex business-to-business products and services – are more akin to chaos with natural patterns than predictable order.

Cisco Systems, Inc., is the worldwide leader in networking—2008 sales $39.5 billion and net income $8.1 billion with $26.2 billion in cash—transforming the workplace, healthcare, environment, education and banking. Cisco prides itself on excellent customer relationships and its product and service offerings have evolved from Internet Enterprise and Service Provider Solutions to other segments including Small, Consumer, and Commercial sectors.

Cisco customers are IT professionals who manage Cisco systems purchased by their organizations; these customers require ongoing, highly complex interaction.

Cisco service consistently strives to exceed expectations and it has succeeded in becoming the Internet category leader through continuous innovation and capability-building acquisitions. We focused on the evolution of the Cisco Customer Response system as a best practices example to illustrate how value network principles could be implemented on a multi-product, multi-market, highly complex product/service system.

To get the inside story on Cisco service, we spoke with La Veta Gibbs.

La Veta joined Cisco in 1995 as Director of the Customer Response Center (CRC), where she had operational responsibility for the front line calls for technical assistance and the corporate operators. She later became Director of company-wide call center strategy and implemented the Customer Interaction Network (CIN). CIN represented a new business model for contact centers globally, one that heavily leveraged the Internet and cross-functional knowledge sharing. She retired in late 2009 as Director of Global Contact Center Strategies.

She has championed the implementation of global call routings, globally shared phone queues, and global web/phone access. She has led Cisco in leveraging the latest call center technology to increase productivity and customer satisfaction while reducing overall workload. During her time at Cisco, she reduced the number of calls, reduced talk time, increased customer satisfaction and increased the efficiencies of routing calls. This resulted in over $19 million savings in four years.

La Veta's experience is useful for all organizations who seek to use web tools and processes to increase customer intimacy and loyalty. She explains how she helped to transform Cisco support systems.

LA VETA GIBBS

Anyone, anywhere in the world that had a Cisco product, that had a problem, it would come to my team's phone queue first. By managing that organization, we developed a lot of innovative processes—this is seven years ago—so we had all of this shared information across each of the product divisions.

We took the best practices in one regional theater, so that everyone could leverage off of it. Anywhere in the world that we receive a customer request, we treat it as a global call. The Internet technology enabled us to do this more efficiently and assured consistency around the world.

We were early adopters in cloud technology using ICM (intelligent call management technology). ICM could identify where in world the next available qualified agent would be to take this call. This utilized our workforce as well as provided an instant disaster recovery path if a specific site went down because of weather or other reason.

Another innovation was to use the Internet as part of answering the customer's question. We could teach the customer the answer and show him or her where the on-line resources were for self-sufficiency, not just to answer the same question again, but also to enable the customer to find that topic and query on the web.

DESIGNING A SYSTEM TO TAKE
FULL ADVANTAGE OF THE WEB

When a customer called and our agent knew that the answer was on the Internet, we would use phone web technology (Webline). After the CRC implemented the system using this product, Cisco bought the company to integrate it into our phone systems. We were the only organization successfully applying this technology to reduce costs and increase customer satisfaction. It was our process and model – not just the technology – that made it work.

While we were talking to the customer on the phone, we would ask him or her to join us in a web session. He or she would key in a code on the web. We would key in the same code and that would lock us together. We would have them bookmark the session for the next time, building an archive.

We could capture that experience (for us and the customer) on the web and analyze it. Do we think it worked? How could that have been different? When did we lose the customer? What were we hearing directly from the customer about that web tool?

Because the call center was using the same tools developed for the customer to use, for the first time we could give valuable information to the web developer. This was a dramatic transformation for Cisco! Because now we were on the same page (literally), providing the same information to the customer. Feedback on the effectiveness and intuitiveness of a web page came direct from agents who used the tools along side the customer.

We could give them real time customer response information about the usability of their tools that they could never get in a survey.

The success of the CRC in improving customer support and reducing costs resulted in a promotion for La Veta to a position where she was able to create a company wide Customer Interaction Network.

Cisco was like most large companies that grew quickly and ended up with many silo call centers, reporting to different business groups and not sharing across to other call centers. This meant we were inconsistent, overlapping and not designed from the outside in. For example, we had five different ways to handle returned materials, depending on whom the customer called in the company. We were all so specialized that, if someone wanted to buy product, not all call centers knew how to handle the caller. Customers were frequently routed around from group to group.

Linking All Customers to All Services

We thought that if the CRC could share knowledge worldwide within my single global organization, then we could do it worldwide across multiple organizations. The vision of having a single access point for the customer—and ability to answer the question or route to the expert regardless of the customer or the question—was called the Customer Interaction Network. It required that Cisco organizations share knowledge and that CIN agents would interact with the customer by sharing, teaching and capturing the experience.

We requested all the call centers to provide information that we put on a single web page for everyone to use. They gave us a question they had received with a short answer or a URL to use.

We could take customers to the URL to teach them—bookmark the URL—and begin a flow chart that we could follow or a form to fill out, anything that would help us while visually looking at it and talking to the customer.

We actually had call centers that didn't take calls! They would just refer the customer to a webpage and then hang up.

Inside We Do Not See the Silos

Another challenge Cisco and many other companies faced because of the silos that evolved over the years was a very complicated and user-unfriendly phone menu. Each time we added a new organization or new service, we added another menu option on the phone tree. It took four minutes for customers to navigate the phone options – and not always successfully. So the clock and the measurement for good customer service never turned on for the four minutes it might have taken the customer to get to the right person. While each call center was measuring what they were doing—a bang-up job—the Cisco rating of "ease of doing business" was lower.

When you looked holistically at the company, and you looked from the customer's perspective, you saw all the silos. None of us inside the company saw the silos because we were so busy doing a bang-up job on our little process. No one "owned" ease of doing business, only "how well is my team doing?"

And so the CIN charter was to make it easy for the customer. Today a customer calls that same number and a Cisco person picks the phone up, using the tools, using the information as provided on the Internet for the short answer, how to escalate, and use a URL. Today, if you call that number you hear a live agent say, "Thanks for calling Cisco. How can I help?" That person represents all of Cisco and will get you the answer or find the right expert. Ownership begins at that first contact, not when it is determined the caller "found" the right group or selected the right menu option.

We changed the name from CRC (Customer Response Center) to CIN (Customer Interaction Network). The new strategy is that the customer comes in at a single point; then we network and interact with the customer, teaching them and guiding them.

Our approach is based on how our tools can provide true Customer Intimacy:

▶ *Virtual: anytime, anywhere, any device*

▶ *Mobile-Multitask: data, voice, video, mobility*

▶ *Global with no boundaries: everything uses a common language*

▶ *Communities: share with friends, peers, experts*

▶ *Personalized-empowered: combine work, life, play and learn*

TURNING CALLS FOR QUESTIONS INTO OPPORTUNITIES

Added to the CIN business model, was a tool to capture the experience of the call (what is the customer saying, how did it go, room for improvement, etc.) Call centers in the past focused only on answering the question but not in listening to what else may be going on that someone in the company should know about. Now it can be captured before it becomes a critical issue.

So we turned the conversations and the calls for questions into opportunities to teach, guide and capture experiences. For the first time out of a call center, we would capture what the customer was saying as an opportunity for improvement. Because we were seeing things at that level—that single entry point—that we never saw in the silos. Before the Customer Interaction Network, the customer would dial a separate number, get to a separate call center—say the technical assistance center (TAC)—and they would complain about order management. We didn't even take a note of that. That wasn't our job. We were sure going to give them the best technical assistance, but we were not so concerned with problems from the other areas. And then the same thing would happen if a customer would call order management, saying something about a problem in TAC. And that never got back to us because we were so vertical and so successful in our silos. It would be lost to the system!

What CIN did was pull the cover back. The CIN front line was interested in any issues, regardless of why the customer called in the first place. We weren't focused only on one organization and overlooking other concerns.

Call centers have always been responsive. We were able to transform that ability to actually change, guide, listen and capture experiences and opportunities that had nothing to do with the reason the customer called.

And so it really changed the dynamic of what a call center was all about. The word "call" went away and it became a customer interaction network. Every agent that picks that call up worldwide is a frontline CIN agent.

CIN changed the ability of the company to hear what the customer is saying when the customer wants to say it. Even before we know what questions to ask in a survey.

TEACHING THE CUSTOMER TO BE INDEPENDENT

Simply, here is how we increased both efficiency and customer satisfaction.

Previously, a customer would call us and we would open a case for them. They would continue calling and we would keep opening cases. In our CIN initiative, when they called, we showed them the webpage where we were going to open the tool. We let them know that they could do it, too—with or without us—making it clear that we're going to use the same tool they could use. So there was no perceived advantage for them to call, but we were always going to do it for them. And they could hear us asking questions and sequentially opening that tool. So they'd go with us the second time they'd call in and they would see it again. And then they would go there by themselves and we added a little "click to talk" button on that tool. We said, "Look, if you go to the web tool first, before calling, if you subsequently need a person, we'll guarantee you'll get to an engineer faster than if you called our 800 number."

Within ten months, we had reduced the number of calls coming in to open cases by 50% because the case open tool was the most popular reason to call. And the customer satisfaction increased because they were happy. We didn't just slam the phone on them, then say do it yourselves: we taught them. It was a valuable productivity tool for them. And in addition, as we were teaching them how to use the web tool, we could provide feedback to our engineers for redesign to make it easier for customers.

The key is that it has to be reusable, repeatable, and intuitive. Also, make it desirable for the customer to at least try to use the tool. Don't force them, but definitely reward them when you can.

TURNING A CALL CENTER INTO AN
ESCALATION EXPERTISE AREA

We were able to equip corporate operators with intuitive web tools so that they could be the frontline to all areas: the technical systems, order management, sales, human resources, etc. Then we added to that so we could have a single frontline organization take a caller to a sales lead generation tool. This is someone calling that wants to buy something. Rather than just transfer them to possibly a black hole, or asking innumerable questions in order to transfer them, we bring up a web tool. And you can input information directly and it's all ready for the sales guys to start working on when they take that call.

So we were adding value to procedures that were repeatable and reusable. The model changed. Rather than having 69 discrete call centers around the world, we achieved truly global excellence from the easy stuff all the way up to the real tough stuff. What we had was single front line (virtual and global) for the entire company that could handle not just the first layer of that call, but had the ability—if the tool is provided to them by all of these other experts—to take it a little deeper. And then that turned the original silo call centers into escalation expertise areas. So they could focus on becoming deeper and more expert—anything that was redundant— they could feed it back in a consistent way into the web for our call centers to use. Using the approach of combining the Internet with the customer while we're talking changed the organization structure. The Figure below illustrates our approach to the Customer Interaction Network.

Measure	Old	New (CIN)
Ownership	Last Transfer	First contact
Metrics	Volume	Value
Customer	My Customer	Our Customer
ROI	Costs	Opportunity
Work Volume	Manage It	Reduce it
Organization	Silo/specific	Corporation-Wide
Knowledge	What They Know	What they Access

Table 7-1 Cisco Customer Interaction Network

For more information check out the Consortium for Service Innovation (www.serviceinnovation.org) a non profit organization for improvement of knowledge management, how to share knowledge and how to create knowledge within organizations.

It is not enough to know the answer; it's not enough to teach the answer. What's valuable is that you can articulate it in a way (visually, graphically, etc.) that anyone can pick up to plug and play. And that's really what we strive toward.

THE CHALLENGE IS ALL ABOUT PEOPLE

Customer intimacy used to be defined as when a customer would call in and ask for Mary, because she knew Mary, who always treated her well. So that relationship was one-on-one. It was our personal contribution to the customer that made us stand out and everybody had to come to an individual for the answer.

Now customer intimacy is when that customer calls in, anyone that they talk to can say," Here is the answer, but let me share more: let me introduce you to my Cisco family; let me show you all of my friends and all the things that they know; and let me show you the Internet and all the other resources available to you." It's a perfect example of the human network in action. So it's no longer just a one-on-one if you come to me and I share my resources with you.

The challenge to make it happen is all about people. Because getting people to share their knowledge and articulate it so anyone else can answer their question is difficult.

SILOS PREVENT EFFECTIVE CUSTOMER INTIMACY

While it should have taken probably a year to put the CIN organization in place, it took three. And the first two years were all about people and those silos that were their own little kingdoms.

When we began to share knowledge across the organization so anyone could use the resource, it exposed shortcomings inside the company. It's very risky and uncomfortable when you look at old processes and data with new and questioning eyes. The process of implementing the CIN model exposed some of the things that we were doing wrong, some areas where we had lost the knowledge internally, and areas of redundancy and inefficiencies. We exposed things that weren't being done at all. We were exposing that there were call centers out there where the managers didn't even know they were managing a call center, because it was such a tiny little sliver of their organization. It was just an incredible discovery and a territory issue; I was like a bull in a china shop. At first I didn't get it. Everybody believed it was the right thing to do but when I wanted to have the frontline take their calls, it was almost like nuclear weapons—not in my backyard. Managers said, "I believe in sharing but not in my area of expertise."

METRICS CAN BUST THE SILOS

CIN learned a lesson on knowledge sharing from the TAC. Cisco has all these really smart engineers. What they knew was their whole identity. If they gave their answers up to be repeated and reused without them, then who would they be? Their answers were part of their value. And so TAC started rewarding them on their answers – the number of answers that they published on the web and the usage of those that were published. And what was reported was not which customer they helped or the number of cases they closed, so much as the things they shared. We also found that some of the smartest engineers were not so good in articulating solutions in a way that someone could reuse. So we created a TAC web team of engineers that understood the language and technical information. They were not the highest level of engineer, but they were very good at articulating for customers. They could collaborate with any engineer who would be working on a problem. They might have just the thread of an answer for the first time or there might be a nuance about this particular case; we set it up so all they had to do was flag that case, that trouble ticket and then pique that interest. And then the TAC web team would go through the files and pull up those cases eventually and then go back to the level three engineers to find out why it was unusual. What should we shoot and capture on film? And so we had to change our reward system as an organization before we were able to really get that information reusable on the web. We focused on making solutions reusable. This same principle applied to the CIN model, where we needed knowledge shared and reusable across the company.

Raising Collective Intelligence

Years ago, my CRC team was worldwide with various call centers trying to answer the same questions in a theater (time zone). So we had two objectives: to be consistent everywhere and to provide the best practices.

I asked my managers to nominate the best agents in their theater, who actually talk to the customer. And I brought the nominated agents together for two weeks to document their stories. We cut out the turf, the idea of ownership, and pride of authorship. So what if all the good answers came out of Brussels instead of Australia? We took out all of those potential issues and had them go through the most common customer questions and collectively came up with what we were going to post on the website.

This put us in the position of sharing knowledge on the website. This was the foundation of the CIN model to follow.

Why Call Centers are the Front Line for Innovation

Call Centers are the first to know that something is wrong. However, we have trained our call center personnel for the last twenty years to ignore or smooth over a problem as quickly as possible and move on to the next call. ("Take a deep breath, smile and take the next call.") They solved it or they passed it off, but there was no focus put on problems outside the silo or outside the scope of the agent. The focus was on volume, talk time, all the mechanics of workforce management. Statistics reflected only time, speed, and volume. This is how most call centers in most companies have operated.

All these years, we have been losing that head start on what's really going on and what could possibly turn into a major issue further down the road. Call Centers know about it right up front. We need to provide the mechanism to capture a potential issue (not just record the answers we gave), and we need to reward agents for recognizing opportunities for improvement, capturing what they hear and what the customer is saying. Build that into the job description.

By remaining silo'd or blindly outsourcing without retaining ownership of the knowledge and processes, we risk losing that connection to innovation. Because the understanding that something is even wrong and understanding how to fix it is key to building the next generation of product. So how do we innovate to make something better? The contact center should become a key player in innovation and must be positioned to bring what they hear and what they experience when working with customers all day long.

This is key for the future of innovation!

WHY MAPPING THE VALUE NETWORK CAN BE SO IMPORTANT

What I'm going to say probably doesn't sound profound, but it is. In first building the CIN model, we needed a new way to view what we were trying to do – other than through square boxes and organizational charts. I wanted my organization to think about our role and how we fit in the company differently. And I thought that the value network mapping was the best visual and process for us to go through—to stop thinking about who works for whom, what your job description is. So I wanted to think differently about how we view our interactions inside the company. And this is what I learned:

We succeeded by getting rid of silos. Making it so that we had a single plan, everyone was pitching in no matter where he or she worked, to be sure we had the information that was consistent around the world, and everyone could reuse it. I felt that every time I saw an org chart or something that had a box or straight lines in it, there were barriers and walls. I wanted us to be fluid in how we were evolving. The Figure 7.1 shows how we mapped our organization.

How the Active Organization Creates New Value via Global Customer Service—Cisco 81

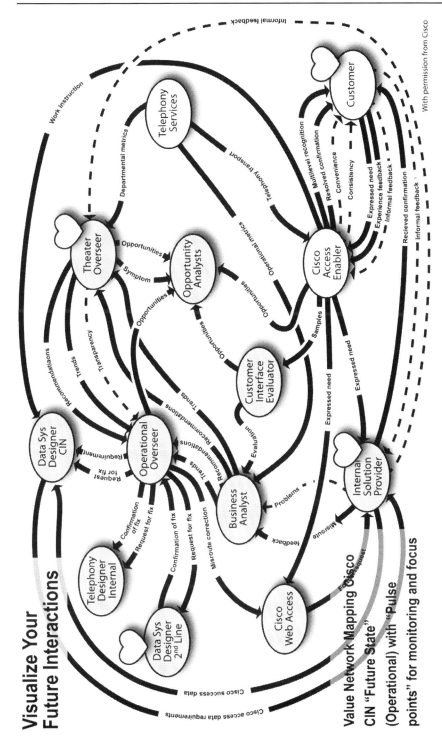

Figure 7-1 Cisco Value Network Mapping CIN with Pulse Points for Monitoring and Focus

It became interesting when we started looking at the various interactions. The hearts represented "the pulse points" for the organization. Everything was going into one place. Is this possibly a place that is a bottleneck? Here is a place that is touching the customer, yet there is another place that is touching the customer. Are we consistent? Do we have the focus that we need to have? So you can use the little hearts and those little markers in a lot of different ways. When you have the fluidity you get out of the barriers and the boxes. Then you can decide how you want to use that value network. How do you want to focus?

EVOLVING METRICS IS A GAME CHANGER!

We changed the role of the call center. Instead of focusing only on workforce management metrics—talk time, calls per agent, after call work—we can be measuring: How many times did they capture quality feedback? How many times did they recognize when there was a problem and let us know about it? How many times did they flag an opportunity for improvement? Could they articulate that a particular webpage wasn't quite doing what it needed to do?

We were rewarding and measuring things that we trained our agents for twenty years to hide. Totally dramatic difference!

As the chart below illustrates, ownership of the customer experience begins with the first touch, not at final escalation. First touch can define what should be measured for the customer experience.

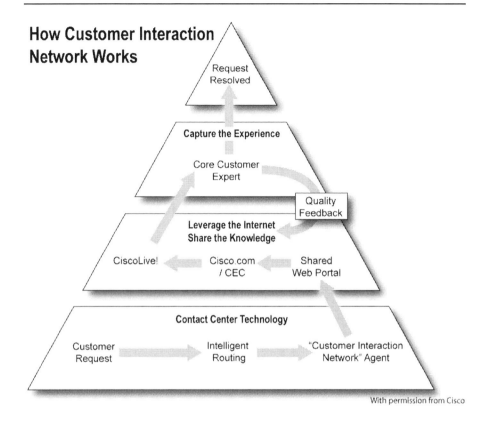

Figure 7-2 Cisco Customer Interaction Network: Changes What We Value and Measure

From Dead End Job to Stepping Stone for Career Growth

Employee turnover in a call center is often because of low morale. Low morale is the result of: no career path, burnout, no sense of self-worth, no power, no sense of making a difference.

The first contact with the customer is their first impression of the entire company. Usually, difficulties within a call center are often symptomatic of deeper and broader issues. So management should take their experiences seriously.

However, our people can be more valuable and can do more things. You can chart your career path to become an engineer or marketing executive. The deeper and more proficient you are, the more valuable you become as an agent on that first contact.

Typically, our area is a feeder pool for the rest of the company. Now the company provides agents with more information. Before they would leave my organization to do that second level job. Now why leave the organization? Why not bring that job to us? And it's cheaper for us to do it than to have that agent move to a higher level. We can pay our agents more if they can solve more complex customer problems. We are bringing that information to us rather than sending our agents to them.

CHANGING THE ORGANIZATION FROM THE OUTSIDE IN

We made this mistake designing web pages with all these different sections—like little silos—based on where you report inside the company. The minute you step away from silos and areas of expertise and focus on ease of doing business, you're now changing the organization from the outside in.

And we started with the first touch coming to a single person and changing it so that the organizational functions with the experts that have the answers are now there. The frontline is no longer just responsible for workforce management monitoring and answering a question and going to the next call, but they're teaching, guiding, listening, capturing opportunities and following information back to the areas of expertise.

My advice to other companies is to stop traditional training and focus on capturing information in a way that can be reused by anybody. Anyone who works for Cisco should be able to use the same tools as call centers use. Any customer that's calling in should be able to access the same tools. That is radical!

La Veta Gibbs teaches us that in any organization key cultural shifts are required to leverage interactions, collaborations, and innovation. Think global, virtual, mobile, and sharing—outside in. Specifically:

▶ Design repeatable, reusable knowledge in a single form shared by agents, employees, customers, and larger communities.

- Encourage participation to evaluate and improve content effectiveness.

- Use the same tools for agents, employees, customer, partners, and communities.

- Assure seamless and easy access, blind to organizations, to CRM databases, companies and communities who own the content.

- Answer, but also listen, teach, learn, share, and capture the experience.

- Measure and reward value not just work force management costs.

- Encourage new career paths to include value exchanges and social network proficiencies.

- Develop new skill sets that include mixed media, multi-tasking, short text message languages.

Summary

- Organizations have to become adaptive to capitalize on Internet tools.

- Customer intimacy can be better achieved by helping the customer to understand and use the array of tools and solutions themselves, so they can solve their own problems.

- Changing reward metrics can drive culture change.

- Product and service improvement through innovation can be accelerated through smart use of first contact personnel.

Chapter Eight
How the Active Organization Uses Social Media in Dialogue with The Customer—Wunderman

▶ How can social media be harnessed for achieving customer intimacy in a silo-free world?

▶ Why is social media different than the rest of the marketing mix?

▶ How can listening become an organizational strength?

▶ How can companies measure social media efficacy?

The technology and consumer adaptation to it is happening so fast that I feel it is important to develop new paradigms of marketing—marketing that is real-time, constantly in touch, responding and adapting dynamically.

— Regis McKenna

Customer Dialogue in the Silo-Free World

For the past 10 years, many management books have focused on customer-centricity. Generally, this has meant gathering customer knowledge and understanding as the first step in the commercial process. Through research and data-gathering by the sales force, the enterprise receives customer knowledge that it can use in developing its communications and solutions.

Today, more than ever before, businesses are able not only to *listen* to customers, they can invite customers to help *shape* the company activities. Customers have input on which products to develop with which features, how events should be planned, and what kind of meaningful dialogue they'd like to have.

88   BUST THE SILOS

When one-way communication becomes a customer dialogue it changes the enterprise's Demand Creation activities significantly. It enlivens, energizes, and stimulates the value creation network. In addition, the efficiency effect—speed, accuracy, and scale—exponentially leverages the communications budget.

However, to achieve these benefits, management must bust the most important silo in Demand Creation—the one separating the enterprise from its customers. Often, companies and their customers seemed to have lived in two separate worlds and at loggerheads, almost enemies. At minimum, they negotiated different sides of transactions and invoices. Salespeople were not viewed as customer advocates; research was theoretical, dry, time-bound and devoid of the emotional understanding that a true relationship requires.

CHALLENGES FOR NEW PRODUCT LAUNCHES

Customer relationship building is even more critical with new product and service introductions that require customer "leaps of faith".

Most new product launches have two customer barriers to overcome:

The Functional Barrier – Customers do not know how the product works, are not clear on its benefits, are not aware of its features, or do not believe it delivers a superior value. Relevant information, engagingly presented from a credible source, is required to overcome the functional barrier.

The Emotional Barrier – Customers do not *feel* right about adopting the new product. They may be nervous about change; they may not trust the new supplier; they may have a relationship with another supplier that they feel should not be broken; or they may have internalized negative information or someone else's opinion that makes them not believe the new information coming from the new product supplier. To overcome the emotional barrier requires the building of trust.

The customer dialogue is most critical to obtain attitude change and adoption to overcome these barriers; successful application of network tools can be part of the solution.

SOCIAL MEDIA DEFINED

Patricia Seybold, author of <u>Outside Innovation,</u> is a forward thinker who assesses and predicts how new and evolving technologies will impact customers. She suggests that the necessity to improve communication with customers requires businesses to completely re-think their contact processes.

I believe that, in order to really understand your customer, you have to know: who they are, what they care about and what they're trying to do. And that means you have to actually see them in the field. You have to do ethnographic research, and go watch them in their jobs and in their lives. You also, in my opinion, have to invite them in to co-design with you, co-design how they would ideally accomplish what they want to do, how they would ideally do what they want to do...

Really engage with lead customers—the ones who are out in front and very passionate about things. Get them really hooked into your organization, and not just through surveys or user group meetings twice a year. And you can recruit and incentivize them without spending much money. They love to be heard.[8]

Today we have new "networked organization" tools to do just that. Now far-sighted marketers are experimenting with ways to use social media tools on a Web 2.0 platform such as Facebook, MySpace and LinkedIn. These tools are now proving their ability to increase customer intimacy through continuous customer interaction.

HEROES HAPPEN HERE — THE CAMPAIGN

In 2008, Microsoft launched the "Heroes Happen Here " (HHH) campaign with their agency Wunderman; it fulfills Patricia Seybold's challenge to marketers.

---

8   Conversations with Marketing Masters, Mazur and Miller (John Wiley & Sons, 2007), pp. 186–191

HHH was a 61-city tour event for three server products: Windows Server, SQL Server and Visual Studio – all 2008 editions. Windows Server is the Operating Systems software. SQL Server is the database software. Visual Studio is software used by developers to build the applications that run on Windows Server or SQL server.

Each event is like a big party for IT professionals and developers. The common themes include a keynote speech, discussions about the release of the three products, and the power of those products for business productivity and efficiency. Break out sessions provide product demonstrations to go deeper into each of the individual products, depending on the participant's role as an IT professional or developer. Microsoft experts are there to walk them through hands-on, individualized product tests.

But more important than the events themselves were the digital conversations with the individuals who were in the target audience for the events. Wunderman applied social media and associated targeting and tailoring tools in an innovative way that resulted in an increase in market participation in the events and an improved dialogue between Microsoft and their sophisticated IT professional users.

What is most significant about this story is how the new social media tools provide an opportunity for innovation in dialogue and personalization with the customer. Microsoft, through this campaign developed by their agency Wunderman, is leading the industry in the use of social media in customer dialogue.

We spoke with Michael Joseph and Blake Park from Wunderman to discuss how social media tools can be used to enhance customer dialogue and build brand equity.

Michael Joseph is the Wunderman Account Director for Microsoft's HHH campaign.

We asked Michael to describe the major changes in communication with clients using social media to reach target audiences. Specifically, we highlight the HHH campaign as an example of innovation in communications.

The campaign highlights how Microsoft is taking a marketing leadership role in offering, "relevant messaging."

MICHAEL JOSEPH
FACEBOOK, LINKEDIN AND THE OPPORTUNITY OF WEB 2.0

"Paradigm shift" is probably an over-used term, but change is real as customers are truly empowered now through tools on the Internet. Companies can no longer just push their message out and merely measure gross rating points or cost-per-impression to determine effective reach as success criteria. Consumers are actively gathering information to really determine—no matter what a company may say or how a company might position itself—what a brand and offering is all about. There always has been the power of referrals and peer-to-peer word of mouth. But technology just makes it much easier and more scalable for opinions to quickly be formed and perceptions to be influenced. Social media, developed through web 2.0 products, now redefines customer communications.

SOCIAL MEDIA DEFINED AND UTILIZED

The HHH campaign began with an intense "listening" activity to understand what the target audience was saying—positive and negative—about Microsoft. By tracking the conversations taking place on the Internet using tools such as Visible Technologies' TruCast, Wunderman can determine the actual language customers use, plus the volume and tonality (or sentiment) of conversation taking place on certain topics, such as what IT professionals were thinking about the upcoming new version of Windows Server. The tool also maps the blogosphere to uncover who the most influential conversationalists are so that those bloggers could be closely tracked and engaged in order to gain scale.

That insight is then applied to the development of marketing campaigns. While the positioning strategy had been developed for HHH prior to commencing the conversational monitoring, the insights uncovered by the listening tools did inform a targeted engagement strategy for reaching key influential bloggers and the development of social network activities.

By engaging with different types of social media—from blogs to social networks to user-generated content aggregators – Microsoft was able to enter into conversations that shifted perceptions and changed behavior. What we found during the HHH campaign was that when a message or content resonated, social media enabled a rapid spreading of that message and content.

In this age of the Internet, customers are reaching out rather than merely waiting for companies to approach them. Consequently, discoverability is essential—a company and its offerings need to be able to be discovered with ease.

In addition to making sure that a company is "discoverable," today's best marketers are embracing the full spectrum of how people consume information and make buying decisions. Audiences are consuming media in a different way—whether through TIVOs or Twitter updates. They are in more control of when, where and how they encounter engagement with companies. As a result, the landscape for marketers is undergoing dramatic change, but at the same time, technology has also enabled relationship marketing to become even more effective.

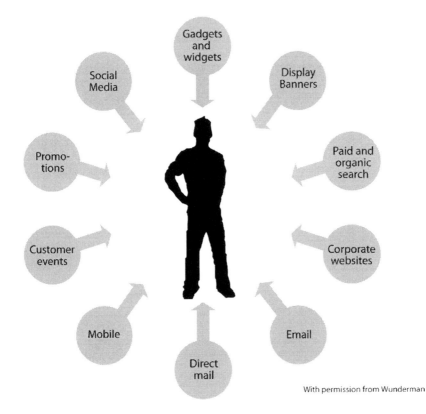

Figure 8-1 Wunderman Holistic Campaign Strategy

As illustrated in this campaign strategy chart, building a relationship-based marketing plan should map and integrate all engagement vehicles to enable a focused and seamless user experience. Such a plan should make sure that all the channels work together to advance prospective customers to an end goal. Each channel has strengths and weaknesses, so the map addresses those so that the customer can advance from awareness to consideration to purchase and use so that they become advocates for the brand. For instance, search gets a lot of credit for being a low-cost generator of purchases or – in the case of larger purchases involving multiple decision makers – of other prospective customer actions, such as downloading a case study or webcast. But studies show that when marketers don't also employ complementary tactics, such as online banners, in addition to search, response rates are not optimized.

The HHH Campaign

The campaign consisted of generating awareness of and attendance at one of 61 events that took place across the U.S. Each event included keynote speeches, discussions about the products by experts and existing customers, and hands-on labs.

The HHH campaign was designed to reach technology users and decision makers in businesses since the three products are commercial software products rather than consumer software products. While much attention has been placed on how social media is used to promote consumer products, less attention has been paid to business-to-business uses of social media. Microsoft's HHH campaign employed social media as a key component of the campaign by reaching its target audience where that audience carries on conversations about technology matters.

The campaign was also designed based on the insight gleaned from research pointing to the way today's companies make technology purchases. Namely, technology purchase decision-making is very much a collaborative process, with multiple decision makers and influencers. The campaign embraced this insight to offer interaction with the myriad of individuals in a target company so that the right people in the organization learned about Microsoft's upcoming product launches and encouraged the hands-on assessors to try out betas and trial versions while communicating the business value of those products to others, all depending on their role in the organization.

In other words, super hyper-targeted messaging to generate qualified sales leads to Microsoft's sales organization.

MAPPING OUTREACH

To engage in social media, it is important to know where the relevant conversations are taking place, what is being discussed in those conversations and who are the most influential conversationalists. To gain that understanding, Wunderman conducted what is called "influencer mapping" of the social media ecosystem. By analyzing the conversations by keywords, such as "Windows Server" or "developer software tools," we were able to find out where the relevant conversations were taking place and identify the influentials (i.e., those blogs and other social media with large followings). By further analyzing the data, we could determine if the conversations taking place were generally positive, neutral or negative in their sentiment toward Microsoft.

Armed with that information, we could then proactively engage in those conversations in a scalable manner by focusing on the important conversations rather than trying to pursue all conversations.

IDENTIFY AND THEN ENGAGE

Proactive engagement in social media is tricky. It requires full transparency (i.e., identifying yourself and your company affiliation). In this instance, it required always explaining that the person entering into the online conversation was either a Microsoft employee or a representative of Microsoft. Companies that have tried to be deceptive in social media—pretending to be someone other than they are—generate negative reactions, often extreme.

Transparency merely required a simple acknowledgement of who was joining in the online conversation: "Hey, I'm from Microsoft, I hear you're talking about this. Here's our point of view." Or, "We see you had a question about the technology. Here's where I think our technology fits in."

Our goal was not to merely change perceptions about these products, but to also begin the conversations with key influencers in order to alert our Microsoft clients about the negative influencers for future targeting purposes. For instance, the map indicates who is talking about Microsoft or its competitors. As you read through the posts and

How the Active Organization Uses Social Media in Dialogue with The Customer—Wunderman

comments, it is possible to ascertain customers' changing hot buttons—what are the concerns, and how can Microsoft reflect those concerns in subsequent communications, messaging or content?

What we saw over-and-over in the subsequent online posts was that people embraced Microsoft joining in the conversation. They wanted Microsoft's point of view.

We also were careful not to enter into any online conversation with our campaign for the launch event as our agenda. If we engaged in a conversation that didn't have a natural and immediate connection to saying, "Hey, there's this HHH event where Microsoft is launching its products," we wouldn't bring it up. We'd just enter in the conversation and participate based on what people were talking about.

We found that by gaining the respect of those in the conversation, we could later bring up the event when the context was right. As a result, we were able to meet our campaign objectives by driving awareness and attendance to the events, or at the very least, have a positive effect on the overall Microsoft brand by evincing that Microsoft was involved, that it cared and that it was "human."

How to Measure Engagement

One powerful metric used for this campaign was the continued action rate (CAR) that measured our tactics through to registration. In most campaigns, paid search tends to be one of—if not the—lowest cost vehicle for CAR, but in this instance of testing our social media outreach program against paid search, we found our social media outreach program outperformed paid search by almost two to one.

In addition, we tracked the increase in volume in conversations about the three new products and the sentiment improvements for each over time.

The Ultimate Focus Group

Monitoring conversational media and social networks can be extremely valuable for marketers. By listening into all of these blogs, user groups and social network conversations, we gain the equivalent of a focus group of thousands. And in many ways, the comments online are even more candid than those expressed in focus groups because the conversations are raw and not moderated. By using sophisticated analytical tools, we can map those conversations to uncover important insights that are then ap-plied to messaging and positioning strategy and even media strategy by focusing on where the conversations are taking place.

The insights can also be applied to sales, product development and customer service. For instance, you can plug insights into the design of your product or your marketing message. You may find out that everyone is talking about some feature, but you have not included it within your paid search buy. You can add that keyword into your subsequent buys. Because you know people are talking about it, they are probably searching and trying to find information on it. This can optimize communication.

Blake Park is Group Director of Strategy and Insights at Wunderman overseeing Microsoft's commercial accounts. Blake addressed how social media is evolving, the issues companies need to address prior to proactively engaging in social media and how to integrate social media into the full marketing mix.

BLAKE PARK

Social media is morphing. We at Wunderman have categorized social media into three basic "buckets" of conversational media. The first consists of the conversations taking place in blogs, user groups and the like. Second are the social networks, such as Facebook. Third is user-generated content, such as videos distributed over YouTube. The lines between these categories continue to blur and shift as new offerings emerge and consumers change their behavior. For instance, social networks let users place videos and other user-generated content on their pages and share with their friends.

The question of whether to jump into social media or not is a tough issue facing companies today. The biggest issue centers on the shift in control that is inherent in social media. With traditional communication's uni-directional nature (company-to-audience), the company controlled what was conveyed. Social media throws that idea of control out the window. Consumers and companies now both have a voice since technology has enabled increased customer control and amplified word of mouth.

As a result, companies that try to wrest control of the message while engaging in social media can find their efforts backfiring. Companies that embrace the back-and-forth, open communication of social media, on the other hand, can find the rewards of such engagement to be significant.

To embrace this shift, forward-thinking companies like Microsoft are undergoing some significant changes—in mindset, as well as organization—so as to adjust to emerging customer expectations and technologies.

By listening closely to what the marketplace is saying, companies are gaining the business intelligence to be smarter marketers with more relevant messaging and more precise targeting. These companies learn by listening in order to use the actual language customers express instead of corporate-speak and respectfully entering into conversations with prospective and existing customers where they are congregating and conversing. And progressive companies also are recognizing that these "focus groups" of thousands can serve as an extremely valuable source for jumpstarting the product development process by hearing how customers are reacting to existing products and articulating wants for new products and services.

For instance, we often use social media monitoring tools such as Visible Technologies' TruCast to map the blogosphere to uncover where the most influential conversations were taking place, so we can focus our targeted outreach to those areas. And by monitoring those conversations, we are able to uncover what terms customers and prospective customers are using so that we can incorporate that lexicon into a variety of communications—from search to email to websites to ad banners.

DOES SOCIAL MEDIA LEAD TO CONTINUOUS DIALOGUE IN REAL TIME?

Yes, it can, and at the very least, companies should expect to commit to social media in an ongoing manner, rather than merely doing a campaign and then abandoning everything after the campaign officially ends. It's much more valuable from a brand-building perspective to make sure that the dialogue that begins during a campaign continues. The nature of the web is that the dialogue is more than likely to occur in real time, or at least with minimal latency between when a consumer comments and the company responds.

There are graceful ways to avoid having to commit to 24/7 coverage of social media. For instance, some companies that engage on micro-blogging site Twitter say that they are done for the day, or are taking the weekend off, so they will reply to any questions or comments the next day, or on the following Monday. As long as you are not using social media as a substitute for your customer service department, engaging with such conditions is typically viewed positively in the blogosphere.

And it's important to realize the conversations will continue to happen, whether or not a company is participating.

WHY BEGIN WITH LISTENING?

Even if a company's intent is to proactively participate in the conversations taking place, it makes a great deal of sense to listen before speaking. A Chinese proverb states, "If you wish to know the mind of a man, listen to his words." Similarly, companies need to listen to their customers and prospective customers to understand their wants, needs and perceptions in order to engage in a relevant and well-received dialogue.

The insights uncovered from listening can be applied to many areas of the company. Marketing gains from better understanding the expectations customers have of the company and its competitors so as to better employ the specific language of customers. It can use that language in its positioning strategy and to developing more relevant emails, direct mails, advertisements and websites. Marketing also can use the insights to identify terms a company can use in its paid and organic search engine strategy. Customer service can gain from having customers help each other solve problems. Product development can gain from the insights by learning where products are generating delight as well as unanticipated pain so that new versions can adjust accordingly.

HOW DO YOU EVALUATE THE COST EFFECTIVENESS OF SOCIAL MEDIA?

The measurement tools and metrics differ from those used by traditional marketing and media. Cost per thousand impressions (CPM) and other traditional reach metrics are not as relevant when you are pursuing key influentials in the blogosphere. As a result, social media metrics typically focus on conversational volume as well as the *sentiment of those conversations, plus the shifts in volume and sentiment over time. Is the velocity of positive conversation or user-generated content being shared accelerating or decelerating?*

Wunderman has also successfully tracked the relative cost effectiveness of proactive social media engagement relative to other media. In the case of the Microsoft's HHH campaign, for instance, social media turned out to be even more cost efficient than paid search, which typically performs extremely well.

And social media can have a significant impact on brand equity. Measuring brand equity poses numerous challenges, but changes in conversational media volume, along with improvements in sentiment of those conversations, can point to improved perceptions of and receptiveness to a brand's equity.

DOES SOCIAL MEDIA ENGAGEMENT OCCUR BY ITSELF?

Given the hype surrounding social media, it's easy to assume that social media replaces all other customer interaction. Bad assumption. First, it is essential to begin with Strategy 101 – assessing the goals and objectives to be achieved – then overlay them with an understanding of the target audience and how that target audience makes buying decisions. Given that insight, determining the right mix of communication vehicles—potentially a combination of social media with more traditional vehicles, such as advertising, direct mail and email—varies by the situation.

Pursuing social media because it is viewed as cool—or doing it without considering how someone reading a blog very likely could go to a search engine and type in a few terms, which then leads to a webpage—is short sighted. It is essential to plot the entire engagement cycle, and then make sure that any social media engagement vehicle added to the mix is rigorously tested for its ability to contribute towards generating business results.

What distinguishes social media as a "brand builder" is that, while traditional marketing is based heavily on inference, social media can be monitored (with qualifications) to assess propensity of customers to engage with a brand and their sentiment toward that brand because social media involves the measurement of the conversations people are having with each other and with brands.

Social media—and the tools to measure what is taking place in social media—will continue to evolve over the next few years. Many surprises will inevitably surface. Think back just three years ago. Who would have expected that the over 35-year-old audience would be one of the fastest-growing segments on Facebook or that a President of the United States would publish his public addresses on YouTube? Admittedly chaotic and filled with hyperbole, social media still offers marketers tremendous opportunity, as long as cultural nuances are honored, so as to respect and embrace the customer; focus on business results is not lost in pursuit of the "cool" and "hip;" and rigor is applied to testing and tracking social media engagements.

Microsoft, through the work of Wunderman, used a whole chain of innovation in HHH:

1. They listened and actually put sensing mechanisms in market—true use of social media and monitoring tools.

2. They used what they learned to then inform the paid media execution. They learned how sentiment and tone were shifting in the market. It actually helped to form content for their events and the way they thought about their messaging and paid media.

3. They were able to leverage their subject matter experts in a very new way. Instead of pulling customers into their facilities to engage with the subject matter experts, they were able to take the subject matter experts to the customers in the environments where they were comfortable. They engaged in very deep conversations, which they know measurably improved their response rate in terms of event registration and likelihood to purchase products.

STRIVING TOWARD THE CUSTOMER-CENTRIC ORGANIZATION THROUGH CONTINUOUS CONNECTIVITY.

Jay Galbraith, noted author of <u>Designing the Customer Centric Organization,</u> has long advocated for organizing the business around continuous customer contact and company adaptation to customer needs. He suggests that the effort to integrate customer interactions and then customize the offerings of the company based on continuous knowledge acquisition is a new management imperative.

Electronic connectivity with customers allows the company to recognize and remember each customer, interact with them and remember more about them, and then customize the company's offerings based on the knowledge of the customer. Most companies, however, have not mastered integrated customer interactions. Interactivity requires the management of dialogues and content across all media with which the company interacts with the customer: Website, e-mail, call center, salespersons, service representatives and so on.[9]

Summary

▶ Social Media tools can provide a new frontier for innovation in creating a real time dialogue with the customer.

▶ Reward lies in increased credibility; risk lies in decreased control of the message.

▶ Social media can be one of the most cost effective marketing tools.

▶ Target customers can be brought more effectively into dialogue through Social Media tools. The result is a better, more effective marketing effort.

---

9   Designing the Customer Centric Organization, Jay R. Galbraith, Jossey Bass, 2005

CHAPTER NINE
HOW THE ACTIVE ORGANIZATION SCALES IN HUMAN NETWORKING—THE INDUS ENTREPRENEURS (TiE)

▶ How does a values-driven organization implement its vision?

▶ How can sophisticated, customized services become scalable?

▶ How can innovation be built into a B2B service system?

▶ How to motivate high achievers to work together as a team—for free?

▶ How to create value through a global technology platform?

Performance leads to recognition. Recognition brings respect. Respect enhances power. Humility and grace in one's moments of power enhances dignity of an organization.

—*N.R. Narayana Murthy*

Imagine a small cadre creating regional and personal wealth on an unprecedented scale in one generation. Now also imagine South Asian immigrants who band together in Silicon Valley to create a professional network founded on mentoring, so their people will no longer be seen as low-level technology programmers, but as capable management and marketing professionals for Fortune 500 companies, able to launch their own companies. Venture capitalists and entrepreneurs originating from the Indus region have been among the most successful groups to reap the rewards of a technology boom over the past twenty years. Their individual and collective success has contributed greatly to the wealth of the region, nation and world.

Silicon Valley formal and informal networking groups band together for mutual education and support. It is one of the essentials for success in this "Innovation Central" region. Paramount among networking organizations stands The Indus Entrepreneurs (TiE). Its mission, structure, and operational excellence—driven by highly accomplished, dedicated volunteers—is a great example of a customer-centric organization that has grown, evolved and matured.

Consider that this organization not only has expanded its regional scope beyond Silicon Valley to many countries, but that they have also opened their methods and network to everyone in their service universe, regardless of ethnicity, gender, color, age, or background.

Perhaps the most successful non-government organization (NGO) of its kind, TiE is committed to promoting entrepreneurship through mentoring, networking, and educating. A group of Indian entrepreneurs, corporate executives, and senior professionals founded TiE in Silicon Valley in 1992. They developed a method of mentoring and networking for entrepreneurs that has greatly improved the success rate of, first, Indian entrepreneurs and venture capitalists, and now any entrepreneur who wants to bring his or her dream to market.

TiE currently has over 12,000 members (entrepreneurs and professionals interested in entrepreneurship) and more than 1,800 charter members (mentors by invitation only) in 48 chapters across 11 countries. In Silicon Valley, TiE boasts membership of about 375 CEO's and 197 VP's/GM's among 1981 members.[10]

TiE Charter Members (CMs) are successful entrepreneurs and VC's who contribute to fellow members and give back to the society—not just by writing checks to charity, but also by mentoring and opening their private network to the next generation of entrepreneurs. The virtuous cycle of wealth creation and giving back to the community is the common value that connects TiE CMs to their members.

Ajay Chopra, Venture Capitalist, TiE CM and Co-Chair of TIECON 2008 (the event profiled in this chapter) explains how many CMs feel about what they "get out" of TiE.

---

10   TiE SV 2008 Annual Report

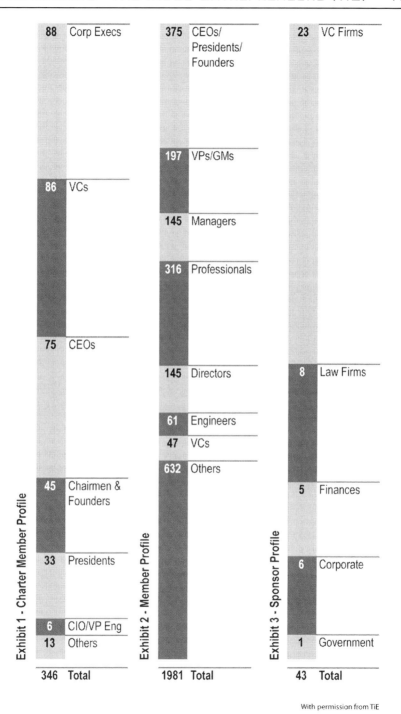

Figure 9-1 TiE Silicon Valley Charter Member, Member, and Sponsor Profiles

I believe that wealth is overrated. No one else believes that, but it's true. Unless you keep yourself mentally occupied, really challenged and aware of new thinking, you will not find fulfillment. My sense is that many of the TiE charter members, especially the ones that have achieved a good amount of financial freedom, find the need to give back and to stay connected to a set of bright young people full of new ideas who are going to form "the next Google."

Meeting with the other TiE charter members is also very important because these are highly accomplished people. Connecting to people, whether personal or professional, is highly valuable. Also the Indian community exerts great peer pressure. Kanwal Rekhi (one of the founders of TiE), whom I have known for many years, would say to me, "Hey listen, how come you're not involved in this?" Now, I find myself doing the same with others. I call a bunch of people and say, "I'm having this mentoring session, you better show up."

The organization creates programs to educate and inspire its constituencies. The flagship event is TiEcon, the largest professional conference for entrepreneurs worldwide, and the focus of this chapter.

You can better understand the success of TiE, TiEcon and their continuous quest for innovation, if you understand who some of the people are that lead TiE and their motivation, skill sets, and approaches to make this work. Their examples illustrate the principles of the Demand Creation Model: role-based functions, creation of value through intangibles, and the drive for innovation through a customer centric orientation.

Raj Jaswa was the President of TiE Silicon Valley from 2004–2008. Ajay Chopra was the co-chair for TiEcon 2008. In their own words, you can see how TiE provides a vehicle for very successful people to not only engage the next generation of entrepreneurs, but to embody an ethos that has enabled the Indus community to uniquely serve their business community, the San Francisco Bay Area and the global economy.

RAJ JASWA

I was educated in engineering in India and came to the US for my MBA and graduate studies. After ten years working in marketing for GE and Intel, I started *my first company OPTi in the semiconductor chip set business in the 1980's. We basically mortgaged our house, borrowed from friends and raised about a million dollars. We sold the company four years later by taking it public with $150 million dollars in annual revenue.*

I met another IT guy, a researcher at Xerox PARC, who was interested in artificial intelligence and Java in the configuration technology area. And he said, "You know, with the Internet growing, maybe there's an opportunity to create a mass market around this artificial intelligence technology." I believed this was in the right direction, different from what I had done in the semiconductor industry, and it could be interesting. And so that one little dinner conversation led to a few more meetings and we jumped in and started a new company—Selectica. It was in the enterprise office space, using Java, and a platform for configuring business applications. After five years, it just took off like a rocket and we did manage to raise a lot of venture capital. We went public and I ran the company for two years, grew the revenue almost 500%. Then I left Selectica as CEO and decided that I wanted to spend some time helping the community and other entrepreneurs. I became a board director at TiE in 2002 and in 2004 became the TiE president and will serve out my term in 2008. During the three years I and the Executive Director Seshan Rammohan have been running TiE, we've grown the charter membership by almost 50%, and we grew the membership another 50%.

GROW THE ORGANIZATION WITH MBO AND PROCESSES

We grew it by essentially applying business management techniques to managing an NGO. We developed management by objectives (MBO) so we had our whole year game plan lined up at the start of the year. And we communicated that to the whole organization.

We said, "These are the projects and products we will work on for this year. Anyone who wants to: come in, comment, and start participating." We generated energy and new participation, because they saw what our game plan was.

We organized TiE to encourage many charter members and sponsors to take initiative to create and run events. Our executive director Seshan, with his logistics, operational and finance background, developed the processes to efficiently run our events and get everything done. Our process was welcoming; many people saw this as an opportunity to get more involved, and to bring their passions to do their own thing into the TiE framework. So we just increased the number of events that we did from about 20–30 a year to almost 65–70 per year.

METHODICAL SPONSORSHIP SOLICITATIONS

We systematized the acquisition of corporate sponsorships—a critical funding source for our major TIECON conference event. Instead of trying to raise sponsorship money on a friendship basis—you know, I did this for you and you do this for me—we converted that into a much more professional relationship between TiE and the sponsor. We developed clear-cut benefits that could be offered to the sponsor. We ask for their help in maintaining and growing this organization; we came up with specific ways in which they could be involved; and we could get the benefits we're looking for. So rather than just knowing somebody at the top of a company who might be able to contribute to the cause, we developed a marketing approach: you find what the need of the sponsors are; who are the people they would be interested in working with themselves in our organization? We have a lot of entrepreneurs and venture capitalists that generate legal, accounting and other business. Addressing sponsorships like a business, we now have a platform for Intel, Microsoft, SAP, and IBM and so on.

HAVING A MARKETING MINDSET

I think the big difference for me was my experience at Intel. The Intel marketing organization has really systemized how high tech marketing should be done: the way products are developed, the way they communicate to the consumer; they way their product is planned for obsolescence; the way they brand it; the way they develop momentum and launch a product. It's a process. I was lucky to be educated and really learn, master, and then teach it to the people who were in my group. While at Intel I saw that even the engineers were permeated with marketing ideas; they were pulled into marketing issues, customer issues, communications issues, and so on. So I learned to infuse marketing into all aspects of the way the company is run and the culture of the company itself.

THE PASSION OF ENTREPRENEURSHIP

I couldn't think of a better job at this point in my life. I'm totally grateful to TiE to give me this opportunity for four years to lead this organization and for this great cause. It appeals to my heart and I love every aspect of entrepreneurship: my interactions with all the professions that are involved with high-tech business; and, of course, with the entrepreneurs themselves. You see the entrepreneurs: they are by themselves; they are pitching their business plan; they are trying to raise small amounts of money here and there. Then in front of your eyes, three years later, they have created a real company. They have business operations all across the world, they are in the press, and before you know it, they've gone public. To see that happen is just a wonderful thing. And as a president for an NGO, I don't take any salary or any compensation. I'm doing this because I just love it! It's a blessing to do something that you enjoy.

WHY TiE?

I like the charter of TiE—helping the next generation become successful. Because once you become successful, there isn't much more incremental value that you get from making more money. And there's only so much money that you can give away. But if you help someone create a successful company, the very fact that he or she created a successful company actually pours so much more money into the community than any philanthropist can give.

We started OPTi and ran it for about seven years with revenue of $150 million dollars and 200 employees in the Bay Area. The seven years that we were there, we probably poured more than a half-billion dollars into the Silicon Valley economy: in wages, buildings, capital purchases and other things. How many philanthropists are there that will give a half-billion dollars to Silicon Valley? And as an entrepreneur I spent it without even thinking about it.

This whole concept that TiE is built on - helping the next generation of entrepreneurs become successful - does propagate the next generation entrepreneurship cycle. You know, entrepreneurs have a very high failure rate, something like nine in ten. But what we are finding is that entrepreneurs who are mentored and who are helped at the right time to make the right decisions have a much lower failure rate, with a much higher success rate for exit, acquisition, going public, and so forth. So what we do at TiE is something that's extremely gratifying. One has a very good quality of life when you are in this mode: being surrounded by people who are motivated and successful, helping others to be successful, and putting a lot of energy into doing it. This role cannot be measured by the dollars and cents that you put into your own bank account.

TiEcon: The Largest, Most Successful Conference in the World for Entrepreneurs

Every May the Silicon Valley venture capital and tech entrepreneur communities converge for the biggest annual event in the Valley—TiEcon. Past keynote speakers have included Arnold Schwarzenegger, California Governor; Thomas Friedman, *New York Times* columnist and author; and Eric Schmidt, CEO of Google. In May 2008, the keynotes were Peter Thiel, one of the VC's who funded Facebook, and Bill Campbell, CEO Coach, and Chairman of the Board of Intuit.

But the keynote speakers are just one of several outstanding features of TiEcon. Panel discussions on trends, continuous networking among participants, and innovative ways to bring entrepreneurs what they need to move their endeavors ahead make TiEcon a most dynamic gathering of thought leadership, inspiration, and practical guidance for the entrepreneur.

Two hundred volunteers who make the two-day event run smoothly served over 3000 attendees. In all, 600 volunteers are involved in TiEcon planning and functioning. TiE has only eight professional staff. Truly, this is a volunteer-driven organization, harnessing the collective talents of its community in service to their mission.

We chose TiEcon, and specifically the innovative E Bazaar, as the focus of this chapter because it illustrates the Demand Creation principles of role-based value creation, customer-centric processes, and continuous innovation in the ever-changing, fast paced technology market. All the more amazing because volunteers—rather than professional staff—define, develop, implement, and evaluate for continuous improvement one of the most complex convening challenges for a very demanding set of customers: the entrepreneurs, VC's and supporting business/professional communities in Silicon Valley.

There are four factors that make TiEcon so successful:

1. The focus on quality: The volunteer leaders tighten all the details that make for a well-run conference, including prompt starting

times, and excellent audio-visuals. They master the logistics of moving many people to multiple sessions, and train volunteers to interact with participants for registration and other issues. There is a lot of coaching and management of the processes, so both the expected and unexpected can be handled smoothly.

2. The focus on relevance: Few businesses evolve as fast as technology applications. New industries spawn quickly, such as clean tech and social media. For each year, TiEcon must be on the cutting edge of changing technologies and market environments. Targeting the right people, topics and approaches that make sense to entrepreneurs is essential to the intangible value TiEcon provides. There are ever-changing success factors in this dynamic, innovative marketplace.

3. The focus on getting the best people on the stage: TiE manages to get the top corporate Silicon Valley CEO's, VC's' and "hot" successful entrepreneurs to address subjects that will be valuable for the entrepreneur. In addition, many panel discussions have specialists who speak to all aspects of entrepreneurship and the current technology marketplace.

4. The focus on networking: Effective networking does not come naturally to most people. TiE leadership helps create an environment conducive to networking at TiEcon. They make a specific effort to get people to realize that networking is expected and they need to be doing it. Networking is necessary for entrepreneurs to succeed; they better be able to network with a lot of people they do not know.

How to Get 600 Volunteers to Work as a Team

To understand how TiEcon comes together, we spoke with Seshan Rammohan, Executive Director of TiE Silicon Valley. Seshan is a fireball of enthusiasm: tireless, gregarious, and sharp. He claims at age 62 he can outwork any 25-year-old. Seeing him in action, you believe him.

Seshan shares how he and his small staff can enable and harness the creative, innovative energy of the volunteers to make TiEcon successful. It is role-based teamwork—facilitated by smart technology support—in action.

SESHAN RAMMOHAN

It all depends on your approach, your confidence in yourself and your staff, and the good will of charter members and the sponsors.

How do we do it? Recognizing good talent, picking your chairs and teams, giving them enough guidance so that they don't go off on a tangent, yet not reining them in too quickly, so that you get new ideas and fresh approaches; having high levels of cross-functional communication, so you can have very good coordination among the chairs; being really on top of all the activities, but continuing to encourage and support people when they've got road blocks. Remember, they've all got day jobs; they are all volunteers. They're all doing this between 6:00 pm to 6:00 am, as opposed to what they do for a living. Being sensitive to that, working three times as hard as the volunteers do, making them feel welcome, and being able to contribute are all part of the management challenge. Listening to their ideas and yet guiding them makes this work.

A key element to our success is the integration of new technology into our systems. We have collaborative tools such as Wikipedia and Jotspots that leverage our capabilities. We have younger people involved; they are better trained in new technology. We listen to their views. We take the 22-year-old guy's ideas and we 60-year-olds learn how to adopt them and make use of them. So that's the power of TiE; we guide and get the volunteer help. We learn from the volunteers as much as they learn from us.

TiE is a Model for Global Demand Creation for Business Associations

The amazing thing about TiE is that we not only have a huge branding and following in Silicon Valley. We get delegations from Japan, China, Korea, Turkey, and various parts of India—now also people from South America and Africa. They have all come to find out: what is the secret sauce? What is it that you do? But they are totally blown away when we tell them: we focus on the individual to fulfill their dream; it's all we're about. We're not here to propagate a technology; we're not here to propagate a particular business; we're not here to promote anyplace such as India, Pakistan or China. We're here to do only one thing. Take individuals, who may have entrepreneurial dreams, and help them in whatever way we can: by educating them, networking them, connecting them and mentoring them so they can fulfill their dreams. In a way, we are totally selfless. It is the spirit of the TiE

How the Active Organization Scales in Human Networking—The Indus Entrepreneurs (TiE)   113

charter members who will put their time, energy and connections and the expertise that comes along with all the wisdom. This is what enables the individual entrepreneurs. Entrepreneurs who are willing to work hard and leverage the opportunities that are presented to them will become successful, who in turn will infuse enthusiasm to the charter members, who are willing to do the same. That is the power of TiE.

To get an inside view of how this volunteer power can be harnessed to make TIECON so successful we spoke with Ajay Chopra, co-chair of TIECON 2008. Ajay personifies how the power to implement an organizational vision, combined with business practices to support the customer comes to fruition.

Ajay Chopra

I have an interesting background because I am an entrepreneur turned venture capitalist—I can relate to both sides of the entrepreneurial eco system. I co-founded a company called Pinnacle Systems and it grew to a significant sized corporation with three hundred fifty million dollars in revenue. I went through the entire entrepreneurial cycle. My company was founded in the late 80's, went public in 1995, and I managed it for ten more years while it was public. I was there throughout the entire cycle and then sold it about two years ago to another larger public company. I took some time off and then became a venture capitalist. My association with TiE started many years ago in the early 90's when the organization was just coming together. I have been a charter member for ten years now and have contributed through various panel participations, but never as intensely as the last couple of years. When you are in a startup and it's your company, you have limited time. After we sold Pinnacle Systems, I decided to get more engaged with TiE. I became a mentor for the TiE mentoring program. Last year I co-chaired the E Bazaar (profiled at end of this chapter) and was asked to co chair TiEcon this year.

What Makes TiEcon So Special?

There are several factors:

It is the only conference that is focused on technology-based entrepreneurs. So if you are an entrepreneur, there's no better conference to go to.

114   BUST THE SILOS

About 70% of attendees are of South Asian heritage, which is not surprising because of the origins of TiE, but also because a higher proportion of South Asian Americans are technically trained, so many more of them as a proportion of the population are involved in technology.

It is incredible that the TiEcon event is put together by 600 volunteers; just stunning how much time, effort and professionalism these people bring to the volunteer job.

We had a post-TiECon debriefing after the event to learn what we did right or wrong and to improve for next year. I was amazed! Several organizing committee chairs presented elaborate power point presentations with graphs, charts, measurements and metrics—to analyze what happened at the event. They had data on where the attendees came from, through which market activity, whether from blogs, Facebook, or the San Jose Mercury News advertisement. I wish I had seen that kind of data from my marketing group when I was managing my company. Here is a group of volunteers who treat this volunteer activity with a level of professionalism that I have never seen before.

HOW CAN TiE ELICIT SUCH VOLUNTEER DEDICATION?

There are two significant elements:

First, is making connections. When you get involved in organizing an activity like TiECon for a period of six months with highly intelligent, smart, well-connected, highly placed people, you create a bond as you get to really know them. For example, I am going to host an event at my house for my TiE con chairs. I did the same last year with the E Bazaar team. They've become my friends and more than one has reached out to me with a startup idea or just to get some career advice and so forth. I didn't know these people before I became involved with TiECon. We just happened to be volunteering for this event together and now we have a reason to connect.

Collaboration with a cause you really enjoy and care for, and being together in the entrepreneurship ecosystem, breeds tighter connection.

Second, is the desire to give back., I got a break to found my own company. It's hard in the beginning. I was very lucky; I had a very successful company with a good outcome. So when I come across entrepreneurs who are doing a startup, I know what they're going through. If I can help them — give my two bits of wisdom and maybe provide some help—that's just a great way to give back. It's far more fulfilling than just writing a check to some organization. In addition, to meet interesting people at TiE who can be helpful to me as a VC is a tangible benefit. For example, I might find one or two very good entrepreneurs that we can fund. So for me, it's more about giving back to the ecosystem that has helped me. I became a successful entrepreneur in part because of Silicon Valley and Silicon Valley is successful because of its ecosystem—the entrepreneur ecosystem. If I can contribute to that ecosystem, I am making Silicon Valley more successful. And TiE is an increasingly important part of that ecosystem, especially for the Indian American community.

GREAT ECOSYSTEM: ASIAN LOVE OF EDUCATION AND SILICON VALLEY ETHOS

Asian Indians come from a very deep-rooted tradition; a very essential part of that tradition is the "pay it forward" philosophy. Essentially, you learn from the prior generation and then you "pay forward" by helping the next generation, or the next set of people who need your advice or help. There are many Indian stories and children's fables on that whole notion. So for people that grow up in the tradition, not just in India, but also US-born with Indian upbringing, it is fairly deep rooted and they learn to think about it at an early age.

Culturally, as is true with many Asian countries, Indians place a high premium on education. You can see that with the attendees at TiEcon; they have advanced degrees, are very involved in academia, and work in knowledge-based industries. They choose to live in smaller houses, but make sure their kids go to the best colleges!

Silicon Valley uniquely has strong elements of the same traditions. Education is highly prized. You do see a lot of "angels" and mentors helping young start-ups. And successful entrepreneurs actively give back to the community. Look at the Hewlett-Packard culture as a good example. A very similar form of that same culture that has existed for eons in India has in fact existed here from the time that Silicon Valley became Silicon Valley. And actually it's a core part of what we call the ecosystem.

These two dynamics intersected at almost the perfect location: the heritage and the thinking of the Indian community with the nurturing culture that Silicon Valley has built over the past 30 years. And the success of TiE is a manifestation of that.

LEADING TiECon IS LIKE LEADING A START-UP COMPANY

We set the theme of "Entrepreneurship: Unbounded Inspiration from the Frontlines." Our idea was that people who have actually "been there-done that" will tell their stories to people who want to be inspired—the Guru-Chela (mentor- disciple) relationship scaled for thousands of conference participants. That objective drove the entire focus of the organization. My co-chair Manish Chandra and I, along with TiE management, treated TiEcon 2008 like we were co-founders for a start up. We selected the best "vice presidents"—12 chairs for each aspect of the event—we could find. Many of them were personal friends, others had been involved in prior TiEcons; we implored them to donate their time and to participate because we knew they would do a good job. And then they selected people in their own image. So the organization was intentionally built with a very clear vision and structure.

Getting the key people in place, just like in a start up or building a company. Also knowing what you want to achieve is very important. As an example, we knew we wanted to attract more people from the Gen Y demographic, so we made sure that every group had a young Gen Y co-chair. It was through their involvement that we were able to attract more volunteers. The reason the ranks of the volunteers swelled to almost 600 is because they actually recruited their friends and said, "Hey, this is a pretty cool organization. Look I'm going to a meeting, I'm going to be rubbing shoulders with important people." So they were getting excited about it. And the word spread. And before we knew it we had an organization brimming with enthusiasm. A terrific starting point to deliver a good event!

E BAZAAR: INNOVATION IN ACTION

Entrepreneurs daily aspire to get the attention of one VC. Imagine having access to 40 VCs and being coached and mentored before your meetings, all as part of your participation at TiEcon.

E (Entrepreneurs) Bazaar was created for that purpose and illustrates TiE innovation in creating value for entrepreneurs.

It began at TIECON 2006 as a simple initiative to give entrepreneurs a chance to meet with some VCs for a quick pitch. They named it "VC in the House." With subsequent entrepreneur and VC feedback, TiE volunteer

How the Active Organization Scales in Human Networking—The Indus Entrepreneurs (TiE)   117

leadership re-engineered the program to become a major focus of the conference. From a few VCs and entrepreneurs casually meeting, VC in the House morphed into E Bazaar, with 40 VCs dedicating a full day and evening to meet with 240 entrepreneurs (culled from 320 applicants), who have spent one month being mentored to each prepare for a 20-minute meeting with a VC matched with them. E Bazaar is a very good example of advancing an insight (entrepreneurs want to get feedback from VC's and make valuable contacts) to an innovation (create a process and forum at TiEcon that gives the entrepreneur the greatest benefit of qualified VC feedback and access to their network and also provides the VC with the well prepared entrepreneurs in their area of funding focus).

Located in a large ballroom in the Santa Clara Convention Center, E Bazaar is an invitation only opportunity for entrepreneurs who have applied, been mentored and prepared to meet with VC's. Each VC has a briefing sheet on the entrepreneur's business. The VC is not there to write a check, but rather to give the entrepreneur feedback on their business idea and ask questions. If appropriate, the VC's may refer the entrepreneur to potential co-developers, to accountants, or to a sales organization. They may give the entrepreneur the opportunity for a second meeting, or refer him or her to another VC. They may recommend that the entrepreneur go back to the drawing board to refine the pitch and the plan. E Bazaar provides a focused, jump-start effort to move 240 entrepreneurs ahead during one power-packed day.

E Bazaar is organized by the TiEcon volunteers to meet both entrepreneur and VC needs. Mayur Shah is a 30-year Silicon Valley TiE CM veteran and Anand Akela, a 30-year- old Cisco employee, is his co-chair. Co-chairs Mayur and Anand are a good example of the fulfillment of the TiE objective to bring in Generation Y leadership under the steady hand of experienced, proven CM's.

Mayur suggests that E Bazaar must go beyond the simple matching of VC's and entrepreneurs. TiE has a responsibility to assure that the entrepreneurs are also briefed on how to best structure their financing with the VC, since this is usually an asymmetric relationship. VCs are well versed in the financing parameters, while many entrepreneurs may be too anxious to get any financing and may give up too much equity too soon.

MAYUR SHAH

What we definitely are looking for is a format where there is openness and sharing of ideas; an opportunity for entrepreneurs to understand the pros-and-cons of what entrepreneurship is all about, what financing is all about, what getting a company funded is all about. We want to make sure that the VC community gets the best ideas in front of them; we also want to expose the entrepreneur community to the best network of VCs in the Valley so they get an opportunity. We want both sides to understand the pros and cons of what they are getting into.

The VCs are pretty proficient. They do this for a living, day-in-and-day-out. In a few moments, they can pretty much decide whether this thing is going to fly or not. The entrepreneurs are typically young people who do not have that much experience. I would say nine out of 10 entrepreneurs come into E Bazaar as their first exposure in starting a company and getting a company funded. So it is very important that we explain to them the intricacies of VC funding. We have seen situations where entrepreneur company founders have put their lives, blood, sweat and tears into the company and they have gotten into a funding situation where, when they sell the company or when they exit the company, they get less than 3% of what the company was sold for. We want to make sure that when we present the entrepreneurs to the VC's that the entrepreneurs understand all of the contract clauses, the funding arrangements, the legal exposure—so they don't get into a situation where they basically come out as losers. Some VC's do not particularly like it when we prepare the entrepreneur for the funding negotiation, because the VCs feel that we are giving away some of their secrets on how they construct these contracts. But it is our responsibility as the neutral party at TiEcon to help both sides so that there is a win-win situation. We do not want to be faced three years from now with an entrepreneur, who says, "I met this VC through TiE and I got ripped off; I walked away with nothing after my company was sold!"

GLOBAL CONNECTIVITY THROUGH TECHNOLOGY

TiE utilizes advanced technology in its operations to help manage events such as TiEcon and E Bazaar. It has developed a resource enterprise management tool to leverage its networking capacity for its worldwide membership.

The TiE Global System (TGS) is a technology enterprise management platform to share knowledge and content both across and within the regional chapters.

This technology platform connects CM's and members, enabling them to exchange information to learn from one another. It is also used to manage the day-to-day running of each of the chapters—44 out of 48 chapters use TGS. The Online Networking Directory connects the 1,800 CMs and more than 12,000 members. There are key performance indicators (KPI) to serve as a yardsticks for chapter performance and establish best practices benchmarks.

TGS is one more example of how TiE is using business process, metrics and technology to continue to provide excellent service while scaling for growth.

Summary

TiE illustrates that business service organizations—even in the not-for-profit sector—can utilize Demand Creation principles to both anticipate and respond to their changing customer needs.

▶ Many people who understand and buy-in to the values of the organization can implement a powerful service vision.

▶ Motivation to give back to society and do well for oneself, as well as others, can be harnessed through good application of top-down management of role-based teams.

▶ Intangible value can be created, refined, and scaled, if the processes are thoughtfully developed—with continuous customer feedback and innovation in response.

▶ Application of business processes and metrics, supported by technology, can support growth and facilitate the creation of connectivity and value, as illustrated by the TiE Global System.

CHAPTER TEN

HOW THE ACTIVE ORGANIZATION CREATES A NEW GLOBAL BUSINESS: BUMRUNGRAD AND MEDICAL DESTINATION TOURISM

▶ How does digital information and globalization spawn new industries, such as medical destination tourism?

▶ How is medical destination tourism a good example of a customer-centric industry?

▶ How do the medical market dynamics of different regions provide a great business opportunity for developing countries?

▶ How does an enterprise management system enable scalable, excellent customer experiences?

▶ What are the business success factors for a medical destination organization?

"Successful marketing companies are those that can innovate, launch and learn."

—Phillip Kotler

When organizational thinking is rigid and static, problems appear to be insoluble. The health care industry in the USA and many Western nations has become so bureaucratic and the processes have become so complex and calcified, that many despair at the prospects of ever achieving effective reform and efficient operating procedures. In the Middle East and the developing world, many who have the means to pay for health care do not have good local hospitals to tend to them. So the global healthcare industry problems vary from excessive cost and bureaucracy in the US, to excessive waiting periods for procedures in Europe and Japan, to lack of access to good medical care in much of the developing world.

Yet, with open and active organizational thinking, with a customer-first attitude, with globalization as a principle, and with an active network connecting locations and facilities directly to information about individuals with medical needs—through digital technology, new business and organizational processes, and the Internet—the problem becomes an opportunity. A new, incredibly creative and effective solution emerges—medical destination tourism. Follow the story as it unfolds in this chapter, and contemplate the borderless, limitless power of open creative networking to solve what was previously deemed to be insoluble.

The principles illustrated by the emergence of this new global industry include:

▶ Putting the consumer—in this case, the patient—first and making patients central to the solution.

▶ Taking a Demand Creation approach that includes devoting considerable time and effort to defining, understanding, classifying and segmenting those consumer needs, both functional and emotional.

▶ Designing a solution for those needs, based on consumer choice, including access, speed, excellent performance, service and trust.

▶ Networking facilities, insurance providers, doctors, information and patients in a way that connects them all together to solve the consumer problem.

▶ Taking a global perspective—just because the patient is in one country does not mean the solution can't be in another.

▶ Transitioning closed loop healthcare business models to "open source" models responsive to increased globalization of healthcare and an evolving landscape of innovation supporting international "centers of excellence."

▶ Responding to market demand by an increasingly information-empowered healthcare consumer. Governments—as well as their medical, academic, research, hospitality, and tourism industries—are well positioned to benefit from "boundary-less" collaborations.

These alliances provide greater value to patients seeking more choices in services, quality of care and destination. Building upon expanded partnership opportunities between physicians, hospitals, insurance companies, travel and hospitality services, and foreign and local governments, an opportunity to create a "seamless" customer service delivery system is greatly enhanced.

MEDICAL DESTINATION TOURISM — WHAT IS IT?

Medical and health holiday destination travel can be traced back to ancient cultures as early as 4000 BC. In the modern world, the practice continues to evolve for a wide range of recommended and elective procedures such as cardiac surgery, hip/knee joint replacement, cancer diagnosis and treatment, fertility and in-vitro fertilization procedures, stem cell therapy, dental surgery, and cosmetic services.

Depending upon the location, procedure, and travel expenses, the cost can range from 10–50% less than in the United States. Any individual consumer, with a need for a medical procedure, can travel to another country to receive medical care that can often be superior in access, speed, quality, price—or all four—than what is available in his or her own country.

The need is quite basic—consumers want better, faster, more economical and reliable care!

The demand generated for better medical services is facilitated by patient access to information on the Internet, an emerging wave of medical tourism services, increasing international medical insurance options, and the reality that the increasingly high costs of US healthcare positions the American industry at a distinct disadvantage to more customer-centric and affordable healthcare options abroad. Enterprising countries—such as Singapore, Thailand, and India - are successfully answering the demand to serve a growing, global destination healthcare market.

Different international hospitals can offer dramatic cost savings for medical procedures. For example, a heart bypass in the United States can be multiple times more expensive than in India or Thailand

124   BUST THE SILOS

(see Chart 10-1 below). A hip replacement in the United States could cost \$43,000, but just \$12,000 in Thailand or Singapore.

Cost Comparison of Medical Procedures

Procedure	US Cost	India Cost	Thailand Cost	Singapore Cost
Heart Bypass	130,000	10,000	11,000	18,500
Heart Valve Replacement	160,000	9,000	10,000	12,500
Angioplasty	57,000	11,000	13,000	13,000
Hip Replacement	43,000	9,000	12,000	12,000
Hysterectomy	20,000	3,000	4,500	6,000
Knee Replacement	40,000	8,500	10,000	13,000
Spinal Fusion	62,000	5,500	7,000	9,000

Figure 10-1 International Cost Comparison for Medical Procedures[11]

In a 2006 *Travel + Leisure* article, titled "The Medical Vacation," the author, Louisa Kamps, profiled medically savvy consumers who are driving the medical tourism trend. One of the medical travelers profiled discovered that "the total price of an overseas treatment—with airfare, accommodations, and even a few days of vacation tacked on—is often far less than the procedure by itself would cost in the United States."

Countries and facilities serving the international market for medical services often provide superior quality at a lower price. By focusing on specific medical specialties, and by investing in education, facilities and technology, they can develop centers of excellence that are unsurpassed in capabilities

---

11   Approximate retail costs, US figures based on HCUP data, international figures based on hospital quotes in named countries. http://medicaltourism.com/compare-cost.php

and results. As more and more volume flows through the facilities, the level of excellence and reputation increases.

We spoke with a recognized industry expert, Janice Gronvold, Founder and CEO of Spectrec, a consulting firm specializing in business development services for the international medical, spa and hospitality industries. She explains the background and trends in this emerging field and the lead taken in Asian countries servicing a global patient market.

JANICE GRONVOLD

Given the extraordinary costs of medical care in the United States and developed countries, it is not surprising that high quality and affordable medical travel is increasingly attractive to new markets. People are seeking cost savings, reduced waiting periods, better quality care, and specialty procedures not allowed or developed in some countries.

For example, hip replacement surgery has long been considered a procedure for a 60-and-older market, but there is now a growing demographic of patients under 60 years of age needing a variety of corrective procedures for hips and joints due to overuse, injuries, obesity and congenital issues. For patients in the teen-to-60 age group, especially individuals with active lifestyles, a traditional hip replacement is a less attractive option compared to bone-preserving alternatives, such as hip resurfacing. Depending on the patient, this procedure can often be a better alternative, more affordable and available in many countries. For patients requiring a complete hip replacement, the price savings in having the procedure abroad can be in the tens of thousands of dollars depending upon location, post op requirements and travel arrangements.

According to research by Placid Way, an international health and wellness tourism company, medical tourism in countries like Thailand, Singapore, Malaysia and India is projected to generate $4.4 billion in revenue by 2012.[12] In a recent report by Deloitte Center for Health Solutions titled "Medical Tourism: Consumers in Search of Value," an estimated 750,000 Americans traveled abroad for medical care in

---

12   http://placidway.wordpress.com/2008/06/16/asian-healthcare-2008-medical-tourism-in-asia

2007, with an increase of six million projected by 2010, and an estimated annual growth rate of 100 percent from 2007 to 2010.[13]

Destination medical travel options, quality of care, and travel arrangements will vary country-by-country, with many competing to be recognized as "international centers for excellence." A good example is Singapore Medicine, a multi-agency government initiative launched in 2003 with the objective to develop Singapore as a premier international medical travel destination.[14] *Partnerships with international medical schools, research centers, and pharmaceutical companies have been developed with the hub of these efforts coordinated with the $300 million Biopolis, a biotechnology research center that also opened in 2003*[15]. *Singapore Medicine is positioning to serve over one million foreign patients by 2012 with projected annual revenue of $3 billion*[16]. *Prevention, diagnostics and early detection are key components of a growing medical tourism market. Another example in Singapore is AsiaMedic, a pioneering medical lifestyle and preventative medicine organization offering personalized health screening, diagnostic services, and disease management.*[17]

In India, significant public and private investments are directed toward hospital developments and specialty medical centers. In spring of 2009, Suneeta Reddy, Executive Director of Finance of India's' Apollo Hospitals, spoke at a Wharton India Economic Forum on current and emerging markets for medical tourism in India. With a focus on offering a value proposition based upon clinical outcomes and high-quality care significantly less than the cost in the United States, international positioning relies on joint industry collaborative marketing efforts. Promotions include campaigns with the Confederation of India Industry such as "Incredible India" with brand extensions such as the newly launched "Experience Indian Health Care."[18]

The New Delhi "MediCity" project is a $250 million dollar collaboration between GE India Electric and MediCity chairman and cardiac surgeon, Dr. Naresh Trehan. Modeled after healthcare centers such as Mayo Clinic and Johns Hopkins in the United States for an Indian and international clientele, the visionary project, in <u>the words of Dr.</u> Trehan, "promises to change the future course of global medicine."[19].

13   www.deloitte.com/dtt/cda/doc/.../us_chs_MedicalTourismStudy(1).pdf
14   http://www.singaporemedicine.com
15   www.sma.org.sg/sma_news/3611/research_bsg.pdf
16   http://en.wikipedia.org/wiki/Singapore
17   http://www.asiamedic.com.sg
18   http://knowledge.wharton.upenn.edu/india/article.cfm?articleid=4301
19   http://www.ge.com/in/news/news_india_6.html

How the Active Organization Creates a New Global Business: Bumrungrad and Medical Destination Tourism — 127

The collaboration will include a number of initiatives to create "a medical institute of world standards specifically in the areas of high-end medical diagnostics, clinical research and development. The partnership will also enable GE Healthcare to show-case this collaborative venture as a global center of excellence and their commitment to advancing India's reputation as a premier destination for both healthcare services and medical research."[20]

Operational utility services like power generation and distribution, lighting, and water treatment facilities will be engineered with environmentally friendly solutions developed by GE green technologies. This venture is the first in Asia, where a leading technology provider has entered into a partnership with an organization in health care services and research.

In Thailand, major medical tourism centers are in Bangkok and Phuket, with five hospitals certified by the Joint Commission International Accreditation.[21] One of these is Bangkok Hospital with four hospitals offering a broad range of specialties, including one facility, the Bangkok International Hospital, designed exclusively for an international clientele. They offer services in 26 languages, recognize cultural and religious diversity, and have country specific marketing campaigns. For example, one of the features in their marketing initiatives to the Japanese market is the option to stay in a special wing designed exclusively for Japanese patients.[22]

Another Joint Commission International accredited organization is Bumrungrad International, ("bumrungrad" means "care for the people"), one of Thailand's premier medical centers and pioneer in medical tourism. Bumrungrad International is another excellent example of a customer focused organization that has established a holistic view of the entire customer lifecycle through acquisition, delivery of services, retention, and referral."

We chose Thailand Bumrungrad International Hospital (Bumrungrad), one of the best global medical institutions, to illustrate how an organization with a sophisticated Demand Creation Plan in resource allocation, go-to-market, and integration can serve the customer through all touch points and provide extraordinary breakthrough growth and opportunity.

---

20   http://www.ge.com/in/news/news_india_6.html

21   http://www.jointcommissioninternational.org/JCI-Accredited-Organizations

22   http://www.bangkokhospital.com/eng/About_Bangkok_Hospital_Medical_Center.aspx

BUMRUNGRAD

Bumrungrad International was the first Asian hospital accredited by the Joint Commission International (JCI), the international arm of the organization that reviews and accredits hospitals in the United States. The accreditation process, in three-year intervals, includes over 350 standards, for everything from surgical hygiene and anesthesia procedures to the systems in place to credential medical staff and nurses. Thailand also has its own Hospital Accreditation program conducted by the Institute of Hospital Quality Improvement and Accreditation. Bumrungrad was the first hospital in the country to be accredited by this program in 1999 and was reaccredited in 2002, 2005, and 2008.

Bumrungrad is defined by the Red Cross with top classification of "A" – defined as "a tertiary care center which should be able to provide quality care in all medical specialties including invasive cardiology, cardiac and neurosurgery."

Bumrungrad serves over 1.2 million patients per year with over 430,000 patients from 190 countries. The revenue in 2007 was US$280 million.

Services outlined on Bumrungrad's website include, "24-hour emergency room; 19 operating theatres; four types of intensive care units (adult, pediatric, cardiac and a Level III neo-natal ICU); and a rehabilitation center. Surgical facilities include two cardiac catheterization labs, 19 operating theaters (two specifically set up for cardiac surgery), a surgical navigation system; plus endoscopy, arthroscopy, lithotripsy and interventional radiology capabilities."[23]

Kenneth Mays, Chief Marketing Officer, spoke with us about how Bumrungrad can successfully compete in the medical destination tourism marketplace.

Ken is a former US packaged goods marketer. His career path can inspire enterprising marketing and sales professionals to work in expanding industries in developing countries. Ken's perspective on the medical destination tourism industry, and Bumrungrad specifically, is a great example of the global opportunities in emerging markets and industries.

---

23 http://www.bumrungrad.com/

KENNETH MAYS

Our success in attracting international patients is due to addressing their primary needs: cost, access, and quality.

Cost: People have a need for affordable heath care; this is the particular case in the US. We provide an answer for some people who can't afford an operation that they need.

Access: For others it is timely access. Some social health programs have long wait times. If you need a knee-surgery operation, you may be put on an eight-month waiting list. You may be in pain, so we provide a fast solution.

Quality: Many people come to us because they perceive that the quality in their home health care systems is not up to snuff. We provide better quality than some regional countries like Vietnam, Cambodia, Burma, and other countries in the Middle East. We have about 95,000 patients a year from the Gulf Region.

Gulf patient volumes have risen dramatically since 9/11 because many of those patients were going to the main hospitals in the US. But they have found it a big hassle to travel there since 9/11. So Thailand is a popular destination for them. Bangkok is a very comfortable place for Middle Easterners. In many cases their government will pay for them to come here for treatment. Middle Eastern countries now have a lot of money. Their governments are putting a lot of money in medical infrastructure, but there is a shortage of medical talent and experienced medical people to staff that infrastructure; their patients come here because they feel we have good doctors.

As a result, people from different world regions have different reasons for seeking out Bumrungrad for their medical solutions.

TRENDS THAT SUPPORT MEDICAL TOURISM

There are several additional trends affecting the marketplace:

1. ***More serious care across the range of specialties.*** *There is a trend towards more interest in heart bypasses, hip replacements, knee replacements,*

and high- end surgery. People come for everything from health checkups to serious injuries.

2. **Medical outsourcing.** *Insurers in the US, like Blue Cross, United Healthcare and others, are investigating ways to incorporate Bumrungrad as an option to their corporate plans. Bumrungrad currently has visits from about 35,000 US residents who utilize their medical facilities each year. Most do it themselves; they take the trip on their own. They are coming over because they are not insured or their insurance requires too much of a co-payment.*

   However, medical outsourcing is different. Increasingly, insurers and corporate clients view Bumrungrad positively. They can save a lot of money by sending a covered employee of the company to Thailand for treatment. So, it's a different emerging collaborative relationship.

   Now insurers are designing plans to offer Bumrungrad as an option. It is completely voluntary. Patients are not forced to go to Thailand for their medical treatments, but they are rewarded for it. For example, if someone has a knee surgery performed in the United States his or her plan would cover it, but they could have a 30% co-pay. However, if the patient goes to Thailand, the insurance company would pay for the airplane ticket and there would be no co-pay. The patient saves money, the insurance company saves money, and the employer saves money.

   Win-Win-Win!

3. **The end of unlimited medical entitlement.** *Subsequent to World War II, large US corporations began to cover health benefits as part of the compensation package for all employees. There emerged an employee expectation of entitlements through the workplace. The problems are: How much should be covered? Should it cover anything you can possibly use with new technology? Does coverage extend to any hospital? Who should decide how much is covered? The employee? The corporation? The insurance company?*

Bumrungrad has a pay for service system; 70% of their business is a self-pay up front with cash or credit card. The patient receives an estimate and he or she decides what to do. It is customer empowerment. The customer is asked, "What do you want? You can agree to the level of service and you can easily competitively shop." There are 140 hospitals in Bangkok. So if the customer does not like the price, he or she does not have to go through their procedure at Bumrungrad. The consumer makes the decision and has plenty of options that can be easily researched on the Internet. If someone needs a heart bypass, he or she can now contact a few hospitals for comparison—just like he or she would do for a family vacation.

HOW DESTINATION MEDICAL TOURISM
FITS IN THE MARKETPLACE

This completes – rather than competing with – the medical market. Many Americans annually travel abroad for medical treatment and it does not hurt the US health-care industry. US doctors are generally supportive. Many are familiar with foreign doctors, having worked with them in training. There is good communication built into the care system between Bumrungrad doctors and the patient's home country doctors, whether it is through phone or email. It is a mutually supportive system: Bumrungrad doctors get information from patients coming over and then provide their information to the home country doctors when the patients have gone back home. Digital communications facilitates this exchange.

At least 20% of Bumrungrad's business involves insurance companies. It is either local insurance for residents of Thailand or insurance that pays for tourists or business travelers who have accidents or sudden sickness when they are in Thailand.

Foreign insurance companies see it as an innovative response to help reduce patients' costs. Blue Cross and United Healthcare are considering Medical Destination Tourism as a viable option because they are under a lot of pressure from their corporate clients to find innovative ways to control costs. Overseas health care is one of those innovations that they could present to their employer clients. Subsequently, as employers are working to control costs, many are receptive to overseas healthcare as one of several strategies to do so. However, some employers in the US are cautious. They don't want to be seen as forcing this on anybody.

About the same number of Europeans and Americans come to Bumrungrad. For some, it is to avoid the long waiting list. For others, it is for elective surgery; social healthcare systems may not pay for some cosmetic surgery, for instance. In England or Sweden special procedures may be very expensive; Thailand is quick and inexpensive in comparison.

BUMRUNGRAD HAS A COMPETITIVE PRICING ADVANTAGE IN LABOR COSTS

The cost of technology like the big CAT scans from GE and Siemens is the same. The cost of the land in downtown Bangkok is not cheaper than most major cities. The cost of the medications and pharmaceuticals are the same.

What is the big difference? Bumrungrad can attract high talent and pay less for labor than most advanced countries. An American nurse might make $60,000–70,000 a year. A Thai nurse, world trained and qualified, might start at $6,000–7,000 a year.

They also pay a lot less for malpractice premiums for both the hospital and the doctors. Thai doctors can come back after they are trained in the US to Thailand and make a nice living. Physicians may get paid a lot less, but they don't have to subtract a $100 or $150 thousand dollars a year of malpractice premiums. In addition, they get a tax break in Thailand.

So, they pay a lot less in cost of living; they pay a lot less in malpractice premiums; and pay a lot less in taxes. In addition, the typical US hospital pays about 30% in administrative costs that is much higher than Bumrungrad.

If you are a patient in an American hospital, you check in, and get all your procedures done before your operation. Often you don't know how much it will cost. You check out and then the games begin: the hospital goes back-and-forth with the insurance company on how much each is going to pay. At Bumrungrad you do not have to go through this.

BUSINESS PROCESS FOR PATIENT ACQUISITION AND SERVICE

Ken reveals how international patients most often come to consider Bumrungrad and how the institution evolved as a major global competitor.

HOW THE ACTIVE ORGANIZATION CREATES A NEW GLOBAL BUSINESS: BUMRUNGRAD AND MEDICAL DESTINATION TOURISM

We acquire most of our international patients through the Internet. They do their research and then they can make appointments. So we get thousands of e-mails a day. That's how most people first get in touch with us.

We also have an international medical coordination office. These are services and processes that we've developed for the last 10 years.

The hospital has been in existence for 27 years, but we have had a big expansion and finished the current building in January 1997. It cost about $110 million, was staffed by great doctors, and had state of the art technology.

HOW TECHNOLOGY AND BUSINESS PROCESSES CREATES A MEDICAL SYSTEM THAT'S SCALABLE.

Ken discussed the enterprise management system that enables Bumrungrad to provide the high level of service it has become well-known for.

We developed our own system through a spin-off company called Global Care Solutions. They developed H2000: a single-source back office hospital management system that combines accounting and finance, marketing metrics, patient registration, medical records and files of digitized x-rays, CT scans and other images, doctors' orders – everything. Everything is digitized and everything is kept in this one data-driven system. This system has been really crucial for our success.

Half of our patients come in without appointments. The average wait time to see a doctor is 17 minutes.

We have 945 doctors: 200 are full time, the rest are part time. Many teach at the Thai medical schools and university hospitals. They'll come over here and work 2–3 days per week. So, we can get this large pool of qualified doctors and match all these doctors' schedules with patients coming in. It is just-in-time medicine!

You have a problem; you come here in the morning; and you could see a doctor, who might order tests and refer you to another specialist. You might end up seeing two doctors, getting test results and having your prescription filled – and it all happens in a day. People are amazed because all those things will take two weeks to get done back home. If you need a procedure done here, it can be scheduled the same week. It is that quick.

Now here's the interesting thing. Microsoft decided that they wanted to get into healthcare and a couple of years ago they opened a healthcare solution division. They shopped the world for a platform and they selected the Global Care H2000 system. They bought the company. So Microsoft is across the street from us. We are a key R&D partner!

BUSINESS MODEL SUCCESS FACTORS

Explaining the business model, Ken identified five synergistic success factors that make Bumrungrad an outstanding global medical institution:

1. *Good doctors: I think people come because they like great hospitals; we have a good hospital brand. Patients look at the quality and reputation of the doctors as a primary criterion. Therefore, we consider our doctors as a customer group themselves. We work so they feel that Bumrungrad is the most desirable place where the best doctors in Thailand want to practice medicine.*

2. *Good infrastructure management: The back office IT systems, combined with experienced management who know how to track the right methods for continuous quantitative improvements, enable us to deliver a good customer experience. So IT, management of business processes, and metrics are crucial to deliver dependable excellence to our patients.*

3. *Service processes: Our staff professionals are experienced to provide service to international patients. For example, we have more than 60 interpreters. Our people know how to sell and service patients from different cultures. We measure customer satisfaction to make sure it is all working.*

4. *Medical quality and safety: We have a very active program, as any hospital does, to continuously measure medical quality outcomes and safety. We work diligently the same way an airline would because peoples' lives are at stake.*

5. *Protect the brand: We have developed a consistent brand as a leader in the medical destination tourism industry. People know about it and they choose us. So, the future reputation may be disseminated by the story someone runs about our work. We cannot afford global advertising, but we can get the equivalent through articles in the international press or programs, such as 60 Minutes on CBS. We can get all this coverage, because we have a very strong reputation and there is high interest in the medical travel industry.*

Summary

▶ New industries are spawned or expanded through a global marketplace facilitated by the Internet that provides open access to information.

▶ Medical customers have the power to investigate, screen, competitively shop, and select medical procedures turning the medical industry into a demand-based business.

▶ Insurance companies and employers have reason to seek medical outsourcing as an innovative solution to rising medical costs.

▶ Enterprise management systems, directed by experienced management, who utilize metrics, are essential to provide excellence for all customer touch points.

▶ The organization has innovated, launched and learned how to build personnel, systems, and the brand reputation.

CHAPTER ELEVEN
HOW THE TRADITIONAL ORGANIZATION
TRANSFORMS — CLOROX

▶ How can Demand Creation work within a traditional brand management structure?

▶ How can intangibles be valued in a quantitatively driven brand management system?

▶ Why do functional departments and brand management hinder a knowledge management system?

Innovation is more than R&D. It involves the organization as a whole and brand portfolio and strategy.

— David Aaker

In previous chapters we've illustrated Demand Creation in cutting edge industries. If you've read this far, you may be wondering if the Bust The Silos formula can apply to traditional industries with legacy organization structures.

Happily, yes! Any company can use Demand Creation to open itself for innovation and growth. At EMM Group, we have focused considerable Demand Creation work in traditional companies, including consumer-packaged goods.

One of our clients is Doug Milliken, Vice President of Global Brand Development at The Clorox Company. In this chapter, we'll examine Doug's story of transformation.

While better-publicized consumer packaged goods (CPG) companies such as Procter & Gamble Company are in the limelight more often, The Clorox

Company ($5.3 billion revenue in 2008) has been a consistent leader in its industry—both in business processes and product innovation. Clorox represents many of the "Main Street" Fortune 500 Companies who have long histories with legacy products and legacy processes. They don't make a lot of flashy acquisitions. They don't brag about themselves at innovation fairs. But the active management of businesses, such as Clorox Corporation, to organize for organic growth has tremendous implications for the global economy. The Clorox Company is a harbinger of the opportunities for mainstream business to thrive in the post-recession economy.

In 2008–2009, The Clorox Company held up remarkably well to the economic roller coaster. It has maintained consistent earnings per share ($3.20 in 2008), EBITDA ($1.1 billion) and its stock market returns have bested the S&P 500 Index. The consumer non-durables sector is usually a safe harbor during an economic recession storm; household cleaning products are staples that need to be replenished no matter what happens in the financial markets.

While newer, Internet based companies such as Cisco may have a natural inclination to adopt Demand Creation, traditional organizations such as The Clorox Company have a steeper climb since they have to adopt new practices within the constraints of traditional brand management and sales systems.

Doug Milliken talked with us about these challenges. Starting in brand management, Doug has worked over the past 12 years in the creation and stewardship of the enterprise Demand Creation processes and capabilities that make The Clorox Company such an outstanding competitor and a consistent achiever. His team is responsible for designing, implementing, and managing the global brand building processes.

The Clorox Company senior management made a commitment to improve their Demand Creation. They started with capabilities—what we define in the Bust The Silos formula as *people collaborating around knowledge.* The Clorox Company management concluded that companies largely compete on their capabilities, and that The Clorox Company could win by choosing a few capabilities the company can be incredibly good at, refining

How the Traditional Organization Transforms—Clorox

them to an unbeatable level of excellence. That insight led them to think about which capabilities are most important to competitive effectiveness and how to improve them. Then they created a process model for the entire company.

Like most Consumer Packaged Goods (CPG) companies, The Clorox Company has multiple business units or "verticals" charged with turning corporate strategy into effective implementation. These business units tend to be "head down," focusing on operational excellence to make the day-to-day numbers. They can't devote resources to longer-term capability building.

Processes, on the other hand, are horizontal. They work across the company's business units and silos. Processes add a unifying, cross-functional capability. The business units can draw on the same enterprise processes and compete on how effectively they deploy them.

Clorox defined one of its "right to win" capabilities as integration in the creation of consumer demand—consumer focused, insight-driven, strategy led, integrated demand building.

For The Clorox Company, consumer demand is captured in their brands—those familiar names with clear identities that consumers recognize as different and special, and which they believe can deliver a superior experience, and for which they are prepared to pay a premium price. In this context, Doug and his team addressed four questions:

- ▶ What are the underlying principles that drive successful brands?

- ▶ How would they define demand-creation capability?

- ▶ What are the approaches and process that they would take to build brands?

- ▶ How would they deploy it to successfully build a brand?

These principles and approaches can be captured in a knowledge asset like the one illustrated in Figure 1. The illustration refers to a standard brand building process we have developed over the years from best practices across multiple industries. Using a similar approach, The Clorox Company developed a fully articulated, end-to-end brand building process that encompasses how they approach strategy, planning, and integrated execution.

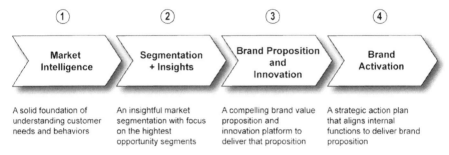

Figure 11-1 EMM Group Brand Building Framework

Working in a highly collaborative mode, Doug's team built a detailed process around a similar framework to make it specific to The Clorox Company to support their right to win in brand building. In doing so, they followed a simple, but demanding, set of design criteria.

- ▶ It is lightweight—the basic depiction fits on a page or a poster or a placemat.

- ▶ It focuses on doing the right things in the right order, rather than on reinvention.

- ▶ It encompasses tools and templates that are extremely user-friendly and can be picked up and used by anyone in the organization with a business problem to solve.

- ▶ It does not live in isolation—it's about people and collaboration; the tools, templates, and process maps are the means to an end, not the end itself.

How the Traditional Organization Transforms—Clorox

And it's accountable! While Doug is the designer of the process, he is also an applier of the process; thereby ensuring that there is no risk of academic detachment. If it doesn't work—doesn't help people get results quickly and consistently—he's the first to know and the first to fix it.

This is an example of a Bust The Silos knowledge asset with transformational capability. It is a knowledge asset built from "what we know now." When we add more knowledge, it can produce different and better outcomes. It can also work with hypotheses—a contingent form of knowledge—because it adds more verification as it proceeds towards the marketplace. A hypothesis proved wrong is a new form of knowledge, as is a hypothesis proved right. Both are valuable. When we add more collaboration, we also strengthen the process and the knowledge asset. Every individual who collaborates contributes knowledge or hypothesis or both for processing, and the asset grows more valuable at a faster pace. Thereby, an enterprise like The Clorox Company becomes a knowledge company, just like Genentech or Google. The difference is, how they monetize their knowledge to meet consumer needs; for Clorox Company it is via brands, rather than medical treatments or search advertising.

Doug explains the brand-building process.

DOUG MILLIKEN

The starting point is defining the brand strategy. The strategy process is robust, examining category growth, the potential for future brand growth, the brand architecture, and the value proposition for all of our brands in the category. Ultimately, we define a specific strategy choice for each of our brands, which is summed up in a single sentence we call the "growth idea." This idea is then cascaded into a series of more specific strategy choices that provide clear guidance to Marketing, Sales, and R&D. As a result, each of the Demand Creation functions can focus on delivering their part of the strategy, but all the parts are integrated around the single growth idea.

Once the strategies are completed, we have a planning process and a set of execution processes to convert our strategic choices to in-market activity. This end-to-end linkage from strategy through execution is a very effective implementation of a networked

142   BUST THE SILOS

Demand Creation organization, all done within Clorox Company's traditional structure.

HOW TO BUILD THE DEMAND CREATION SYSTEM

Designing the process is only the starting point, and in many respects, the easiest part of becoming a process driven organization. The bigger challenge is implementing the process and ensuring that it delivers and lives over time. Our solution to this challenge has been to identify dedicated people to become the owners of the processes. Each owner is essentially the brand manager of that process. His or her role is to create the process, to deploy it, train others in that process, and to generate metrics to understand how well it's working.

Dedicated process owners must have the interest and aptitude to do this kind of work; it's not for everybody, because the work is quite conceptual. Brand building is not a transactional process; it's really a knowledge process. We're trying to answer the ever-changing question: What grows brands? We have to create a set of principles with abstract conceptual thinking, but then eventually get it down to a concrete level of action, and then train people at a level of specificity about exactly what they are supposed to do.

Finding the right people is really important; the next challenge is to provide them with measurable objectives. Therefore, for the process owners we have been able to define a very clear set of objectives for each of these processes. Their objectives might be less specific than most marketers are used to – since we are not delivering a volume target, a market share target, a profit target—but they are no less measurable and no less important or fundamental. This work is about intangibles. We're delivering change and progress and effective tools.

HOW TO VALUE INTANGIBLES IN A QUANTITATIVELY DRIVEN BRAND MANAGEMENT SYSTEM

While The Clorox Company is evolving, we do use the brand management structure. My role and my colleagues' roles at the corporate level are designed to be complementary to the traditional brand management structure. A brand manager is responsible for the business: budget decisions and the results sit in the business unit with those teams. The decision rights of my team at the corporate level are in regard to the process *that the company and all its brand teams are going to use to do brand building. We say, "Look, if you have to do a brand-strategy project, you can sit around for three days and try to design how you're going to go through that process, but that's a waste of your time. What we need you to be thinking about are the solutions for the business. So we have developed the best process for how to do this work. We will coach and train you on how to go through the process."*

Since our role is an enabling one, the challenge for the process owner is measuring the value and impact of that process on the business. How do you demonstrate to company management that a particular process or capability has driven an improved business result either on a specific business or across the entire portfolio? We've actually made some progress here. We can measure if a business has been through the process, and if we think, judgmentally, that they've done the work in a "best practice way." We can also measure the results of those brands that have followed the process vs. those that haven't. We can demonstrate numerically and objectively that brands that have been through the process significantly outperform those that haven't.

A CHALLENGE TO BECOMING A KNOWLEDGE-BASED COMPANY: TRADITIONAL ORGANIZATION STRUCTURES HINDER DEVELOPMENT OF A KNOWLEDGE MANAGEMENT SYSTEM.

The Bust The Silos approach to business growth revolves around knowledge. Therefore, it is logical that investment in knowledge management systems is critical to support opening the organization for organic growth. For example, in Chapter 6 we demonstrate how knowledge management can be used to accelerate informal learning in Genentech through the practice of using experts to answer questions that can be posted and archived for the sales force.

Doug Milliken understands how helpful a robust, constantly improving knowledge management system can be for a traditional organization like The Clorox Company. But he has also experienced how difficult it is to implement in the legacy culture of brand management. He explains why:

Companies like ours do not have a history of developing very robust knowledge management systems. While we do have KM software applications, and are in the midst of developing more advanced systems, we likely lag web-centric and web-facilitated companies like Cisco. We don't yet have common digital work processes that ask the brand teams to simply fill in the information that is readily available in usable formats.

One root of the problem is that, traditionally, the brand group was structured as the "hub of the wheel." It was the central switchboard that every other function in the company had to go through for anything that concerned the brand, wherever they were in the value chain. The Brand Manager was the "mini general manager of the business." Therefore, all brand information and all activity were highly centralized within the brand group and brand managers would tightly hold information.

Today, the brand management function has evolved from the hub of the wheel to a key orchestrator in the Demand Creation Network. Our organization is trying to be better integrated, so that marketing, sales, and R&D are working together as a team. Everyone has particular roles calling for more information, and more accessibility to more people, more broadly shared.

You now need a whole culture around information sharing and how to maintain it. Getting there is hard because the business case for knowledge management is not easy to assemble. Also, applying process thinking to knowledge work is more difficult. Most people understand that transactional systems (such as sales orders) require a process and technology enablement. But the concept of a knowledge process and knowledge management for brand building or innovating is still a conceptual frontier— senior management must drive it.

SENIOR MANAGEMENT LEADERSHIP IS KEY TO ESTABLISHING THE DEMAND CREATION PROCESS

Our management believes that companies compete and win in large part based on their capabilities. If they can excel in a few chosen capabilities, they can win. For example, P&G may excel in R&D; GE may excel in developing leaders and allocating capital.

Years back, our executive team understood that to become a more capable organization our future was not only about job or department functions, but would also be about work process. Functions supply functional or technical expertise, and develop people; processes define how everyone works together to get the work done and deliver value.

How the Traditional Organization Transforms—Clorox 145

So management led the initiatives to move to a process oriented approach and to define the core processes of the company.

They appointed leaders for each of those processes to develop, nurture and manage those processes. These are great challenges: both the intellectual challenge of developing and establishing new processes, and then a gigantic cultural change to shift the company's thinking to the new way. You can never succeed by taking a bottom-up approach to becoming a more process-driven company. Why? Because you must rethink the way the whole company operates. You have to change job definitions, you have to change the nature of the work, you have to add new organizational pieces, and you've got to do all of it simultaneously. You simply can't do all that from the bottom up.

The Clorox Company—a good example of a brand management system—is committed to adapting to Demand Creation. However, as Doug Milliken has explained, it requires determined and visionary leadership to bust the silos!

Summary

▶ Demand Creation is an example of organizing for organic growth.

▶ It can be applied to brand building in consumer packaged goods through the application of process and cross-functional integration between process owners and brand management.

▶ Careful measurement can establish how processes contribute to increasing market share growth.

▶ Long-established companies with legacy systems have structural and cultural barriers that make Demand Creation adoption more difficult than in newer companies.

▶ One such barrier is the slow development of shared knowledge systems and technology-enabled collaboration around knowledge.

▶ Senior management commitment is essential for Demand Creation adoption.

AFTERWORD

We have focused on the organization and how it must change to succeed. Demand Creation will be the leading edge of organizational change in this era and we hope our work has contributed to the dialogue and understanding of best practices toward that end.

In addition to the transformation of the organization there is a global attitudinal transformation in the way in which many young people approach the workplace that we have touched upon only briefly in this book.

The Economist Jeremy Rifkin (Age of Access, 2000) foresaw a shift in psychology to an experiential culture:

We are making a long-term shift from industrial production to cultural production. The meteoric rise of the entertainment economy bears witness to a generation in transition from accumulating things to accumulating experiences.

At EMM Group we witnessed this transformation first hand during some Demand Creation work we were conducting in Moscow. We were studying the attitudes and desires of young people who had recently moved from the suburbs to the big city. They had worked hard to make the move, at some personal risk, since Moscow is the bright light that attracts many moths, but does not always make it easy for new arrivals to adapt, settle and succeed.

We expected to find the striving attitude to continue once these young workers had made it to the big city. But our research data showed something different. The striving was gone. Our research subjects were not driving hard to climb the corporate and social ladder. They did not appear to be motivated by the usual kind of career achievement and status symbols. Spending time with their friends, going to the latest disco or club, and investing their time in digital social networking software and YouTube, was preferred to spending time on burnishing their career achievements.

Evaluating this behavior by our 20th century corporate values, we were beginning to think that this cohort of consumers—for all their energy and creativity and style—were lazy and unwilling to work hard enough to hit the milestones of achievement.

Happily, we were enlightened. A brave and astute young Russian in the workshop stood up and shouted, "You don't understand!"

"You see what you think is lack of drive for achievement. But an achievement defined by their superiors in a hierarchy is no achievement at all. The achievement they strive for is *to do something creative and unexpected that is noticed by their peers.*"

A striking revelation! This is relevant for young people all over the world, not just in Russia. They will invest energy, pursue breakthrough ideas, and strive for self-expression through creativity. But they will not do so within the structures that the previous generations have put in place. They will not be motivated by the same rewards of vertical promotion—granted by their superiors—within a silo'd hierarchy. Instead, they will use new tools of collaboration to create new ways to achieve the reward of being noticed by their peers. They will achieve new forms of balance in their lives. They will judge themselves by new norms of achievement.

This culture will shape the nature of business organizations rather than the other way round. There is no limit to the creative output of this new generation and their 21st century infrastructure of collaborative networking. Unless, that is, we attempt to constrain them in a 20th century organizational concept and burden them with the rules of an outmoded structure. If unleashed, they will create new solutions. If constrained, they will simply migrate to a freer place. Our task as organizers of the 21st century economy is to turn loose this collaborative energy so they may create customer centric organizations and services we cannot even conceive.

ABOUT THE AUTHORS

Hunter Hastings is Chairman of EMM Group, a trailblazing consultancy in the field of Demand Creation. With Jeff Saperstein, Hunter has co-authored The New Marketing Mission, which chronicles the impact of process, metrics and technology on the field of marketing, and Improve Your Marketing To Grow Your Business, a book which demonstrates the linkages of investments in Demand Creation to business results. Hunter and his company provide consulting services to global clients in the Americas, Asia and Europe.

Jeff Saperstein is an author, teacher, consultant, and enabler in how technology can be used to create growth in regional economic development and success for organizations.

His books and case studies are focused upon best practices for innovation. "Toyota: Driving the Mainstream Market to Purchase Hybrid Electronic Vehicles" is one of Richard Ivey Business School top ten most popular case studies.

He has worked with governments, corporations, and NGO's to use marketing to increase growth. Jeff teaches writing and speaking at San Francisco State University College of Business and on-site at Cisco and other corporations. He teaches seminars on Tech Clusters and Innovation at the European School of Management in Paris.

Jeff also hosts International MBA groups for immersion tours in Silicon Valley and leads technology bloggers on writing trips to regional centers of innovation excellence including Israel and London/Cambridge.

Website: http://www.creatingregionalwealth.com/

Jeff lives in Mill Valley, California with his wife, Ilene Serlin.

Made in the USA
Lexington, KY
11 November 2010